The World
Is My Cloister

The World
Is My Cloister

Living from the Hermit Within

~

John Michael Talbot

ORBIS BOOKS

Maryknoll, New York 10545

Third Printing, February 2011

Founded in 1970, Orbis Books endeavors to publish works that enlighten the mind, nourish the spirit, and challenge the conscience. The publishing arm of the Maryknoll Fathers and Brothers, Orbis seeks to explore the global dimensions of the Christian faith and mission, to invite dialogue with diverse cultures and religious traditions, and to serve the cause of reconciliation and peace. The books published reflect the views of their authors and do not represent the official position of the Maryknoll Society. To learn more about Maryknoll and Orbis Books, please visit our website at www.maryknollsociety.org.

Published by Orbis Books, Maryknoll, New York 10545–0302.

Manufactured in the United States of America.
Manuscript editing and typesetting by Joan Weber Laflamme.

Library of Congress Cataloging-in-Publication Data

Talbot, John Michael.
    The world is my cloister : living from the hermit within / John Michael Talbot.
       p. cm.
    Includes bibliographical references and index.
    ISBN 978–1–57075–858–4 (pbk. : alk. paper)
    1. Spiritual life—Christianity. 2. Christian life. I. Title.
    BV4501.3.T35 2010
    248—dc22
                                      2009028414

To Mike Leach,
my first and favorite editor
and my good friend

Contents

Preface

*The world is my cloister, my body is my
cell, and my soul is the hermit within.*

—SAINT FRANCIS OF ASSISI

Saint Francis of Assisi (1181–1226) said those words more
than eight hundred years ago. And they are as powerful today
as they were when he found God in the valleys of Umbria.
That was the inspiration for Francis to found a religious order
known for its love of life, appreciation of silence, and authentic preaching to those who live in towns and cities. A popular
story says that when an eager young friar told Francis he
couldn't wait to leave the cloister and spread the gospel to the
world, Francis smiled at him and said: "We must preach the
good news at all times. If necessary, we use words."

That was then, and this is now. Yet each of us has an inner
hermit that speaks louder than words, and calls for us to be
still. The inner hermit is that part of our soul that longs for
silence in a noisy world, hungers for peace, and bears witness,
with or without words, to "the peace of Christ that passes all
understanding" (Col 3:15).

We hear this divine monastic call to love life, appreciate
silence, and express truth, goodness, and beauty simply because we are human. And we benefit whenever we take the
time to *listen* to the voice that lies deep within. As Jesus said,
peace of heart comes when we are "in the world, but not of
the world" (Jn 1:13).

Would you like to know and express that peace in your own life? Did you know that you can be a hermit and live in a skyscraper and work in a bank? Whether you live in a crowded city or a rural area, work in an office or on a truck or at home, are single or married, with or without children, you can discover your own inner hermit and become a healing presence in this world.

Making the world your cloister by living from the hermit within is what this book is about.

A New Pentecost

*What has been will be again, what has
been done will be done again; there is
nothing new under the sun.*

—Ecclesiastes *1:9–14, NIV*

You may be surprised to learn that people who express the
spirit of monastic orders while living in the world are multiply-
ing like loaves and fishes.

Fact is, while membership in the residential celibate monastic community of monks or nuns is decreasing, the numbers of
those who associate with the monastery while living in the
midst of a secular society are rising. This phenomenon has
been happening at least for the last ten years.

There are many names for these individuals. They are called
oblates among Benedictines; seculars among Franciscans,
Dominicans, and Carmelites; and associates or affiliates among
myriad other communities. In the Brothers and Sisters of Charity we call them domestics, from the Latin *domus,* meaning
"home," not because they clean up or cook but because, wherever they make their "nest," they express the most fundamental meaning of church as lived out at Little Portion. Whatever
the name, the phenomenon is similar. Men and women who
live in the secular world find great strength in living from their
"hermit within" through associating with monastic communities. I am reminded of Saint Bonaventure's prophecy in the
fourteenth century of a contemplative church of the future,

and a new Seraphic Order made up of true contemplatives from all religious and monastic communities—and every state of life. These individuals today are endeavoring to be leaven to the world by embodying time-tested values that transcend the world.

Their numbers promise to grow. Most monastic communities are finding that growth among associates is matching the numbers of the celibate monastic community by ten or twenty to one. So the numbers of those who live in monasteries is likely to continue going down while the numbers of associates or affiliates or domestics will radically increase.

This sounds good, and is good, but the phenomenon could also be troublesome. It begs a big question: What happens when there are no longer enough monks or nuns to operate the monastery? Who will be left to associate *with*? This is a valid question, with some difficult answers.

First of all, why is this happening? In some ways the loss of celibate monastic vocations is indicative of a Western culture that finds lifelong commitment to almost anything impossible. Whether marriage or a call to radical gospel communities, Americans find anything more than a few years too much to promise. Most of us do not persevere in lifelong commitments. When it comes to spiritual communities like hermitages and monasteries, it is one thing to make a commitment from the familiarity of our own private space with minimal time commitment. It is quite another to make a commitment that requires a complete change of our life and lifestyle. Some would say that this lack of lifelong commitment is typical of Western society in general.

But others would see the glass filling to the top with new water and say that the new phenomenon of associates and affiliates of monastic communities is a necessary stage in the evolution of consecrated life. They say that all but a few of the oldest and strongest monasteries and communities must inevitably pass away. Then rising up in Christ—as the legendary phoenix rises from its own ashes—new communities will be born from the lay expressions of consecrated or monastic life. Some see this change coming to fruition in the next decade as the older members of residential monastic communities begin to get sick and die. Indeed, we may see numerous monasteries across America with a mere handful of members running a religious institution built for one or two hundred.

Whether or not this scenario is correct, the current phenomenon of individuals who live away from a monastic building but associate with a monastic order and live holy, productive lives is simply too big to write off as a spiritual fad. There is something holy and wholesome in it. Those who appreciate the values of monastic and consecrated communities are finding themselves greatly helped in their spiritual life by such an association.

But there is more, much more. For every person who joins as an oblate, secular, domestic, or associate, there are hundreds, perhaps even thousands, more who find inspiration from simply reflecting on the hermitical and monastic saints and movements. This is a totally indefinable and innumerable group of folks just trying to make it through the day without totally losing their spiritual footing or perhaps just now finding it. They are Catholics and non-Catholics, Christians and non-Christians, believers and unbelievers. In a way this is a new Pentecost, an event of the Holy Spirit firing people's desire for God. I hope this book can bring some knowledge and inspiration to those interested in either pursuing the path as an associate or learning about the spiritual values in monastic life that they can apply to their own lives on their own.

This phenomenon echoes the beautiful phrase coined by Cardinal Leon Joseph Suenens of Belgium after the Second Vatican Council: a new Pentecost. "Be of courage," he wrote. "The power of the Holy Spirit is at work deep within the heart of the church, breathing into it a fresh youthfulness. It is the Spirit who is our living hope for the future."

I write this book from my own experience as founder and member of the Brothers and Sisters of Charity at Little Portion Hermitage, one of these new communities, nestled in the Ozark Mountains near Eureka Springs, Arkansas, with associates throughout the country. We are an integrated monastic community of celibates, singles, and families. We also have a domestic expression for those who live in their own homes. I am a family member at Little Portion, sharing this way of life and our small hermitage with my wife, Viola, a co-founder. During these decades in community I have served as general minister, but I mainly consider my role as spiritual father and teacher as the job description for my role in community. But I do have a hermit's heart. For the past five years I have been given permission from the community and my spiritual director to transfer to first three and then five days of religious reclusion a week in my small mountain hermitage.

As an integrated monastery Little Portion incorporates the intense community life of normative monasticism seen with the Benedictines; the graduated solitude of Carthusian, Carmelite, and Franciscan monasticism; and the strict reclusion of the Camaldolese. This book has its sources in all these great traditions.

These traditions give authority and confirmation to what you may be hearing in your heart. The voice of the hermit within you is not misplaced zeal. We are all part of a stream of spirituality that is both ancient and new. The traditions, ever growing and changing, give us universal pointers to our ultimate destination: union with God through Jesus Christ.

In this book we will take a journey then, to better understand what we need to know to make the world our cloister, to live life from our hermit within. It is a journey through space and time that leads to a place beyond space and time. It is a journey guided by many mystical and monastic traditions. It is also a journey that is quite personal, as I share a bit from my own experience as a founder and spiritual father of a new integrated monastic community in the United States with associates from New York to California.

In my spiritual life I have found great inspiration in the gospel of Jesus Christ and the many monastic traditions in the church. I have found fiery zeal in the way of Saint Francis of Assisi, evangelical purity in the Rule of Saint Basil, and the call to common life from the Rule of Saint Augustine. I also carry a deep love for the hermit traditions of Saint Antony of the Desert; Saint Romuald, the founder of the Camaldolese; and Saint Bruno, the founder of the Carthusians. But when it comes to day in and day out practical wisdom of how to live in community, I find the Rule of Saint Benedict the most helpful.

"But you are a Franciscan, aren't you?" people ask. "You wear brown a lot." Well, yes, I do, but there's more. Little Portion is spiritually born of a Franciscan mother, but it has become something unique and new for our time. It is an expression of that new spiritual movement of laity, diocesan clergy, and those of all faiths seeking to be associated with religious, monastic communities. In religious terms they are devoted to expressing the values of their spiritual home and family wherever they happen to hang their clothes. They are people who find encouragement and inspiration in the consecrated and monastic community that speaks to their individual hermit within.

So then, let's get started and look first at who and where we are and then at some of the spiritual traditions, values, and practices that will get us to the place where we can see the world as our cloister.

Body, Soul, and Spirit

~

Who is it that seeks peace, solitude, and stillness? Why pray or meditate? Why embrace any spiritual discipline? What is the deeper question?

Who am I?

Sorry, Hamlet, but *that* is the question.

And that question was the mantra-like prayer of Saint Francis: "Lord, who am I, and who are you?" It was the basic question behind the entire spirituality of Ramana Maharshi, the great Indian holy man of the twentieth century. Both men believed that this question led to all insights about the God "in whom we live and move and have our being" (Acts 17:28). In truth, that is where we are all the time. The purpose of monastic spirituality is to know it and be there with all our heart and mind.

So then, who are we? In his first letter to the Thessalonians, Saint Paul describes a human being as "whole and entire, spirit, soul, and body" (1 Thes 5:23). What are these elements, and how do they affect where we live and move and have our being?

Let's take them from the bottom up. *Body* is the sensual aspect of our being. It includes the five traditional senses. In light of modern medicine it also includes the emotions, since so many of our emotional reactions are chemical, and is related to the brain, which releases chemicals as a result of thought. *Soul* is more than thoughts or reasoning. It is awareness and spiritual cognition. Many medieval theologians used mind and soul interchangeably. These are our perceptible energies. *Spirit* is the essence of our very being. It is the core of who we are. The Eastern Christian fathers taught that the spirit is able to exist beyond the boundaries of space and time, beyond body and soul. The spirit exists beyond the beyond, yet it permeates everything. It can only be known through pure spiritual intuition that is beyond thoughts, feelings, or senses but includes them all. As Saint Paul said, we are "whole and entire."

Here is an example of how these elements affect us. A few months ago my wife, Viola, slipped in the bathroom and cracked her head on the side of the sink. I heard the noise and rushed in. When I saw the blood, my emotions turned my body cold. My thoughts of her being injured turned into fear. Body acted on soul or mind, and soul or thought became body. It was impossible to tell which was which. It was only later, when I was able to reflect on who and where Viola really was, a spiritual child of God in the embrace of God, that calm and peace and assurance took the place of fearful thoughts, emotions, and bodily reactions.

Of course, later I entertained the fearful thought that maybe she'd be permanently brain damaged, and the same crazy reactions set in. Needless to say, Viola got it right from the start. She just lay back and trusted in God. She knew at a deeper level than I did that who we really are is *spirit*.

God's essence or spirit is our essence because we "are made in the image and likeness of God" (Gn 1:26). God is beyond all sensual perception, all emotion, and all thought. We can discern the movement of the Spirit in form, but in essence God is beyond all appearance. The Christian mystics taught that this quality of God can be known only through "unknowing." When we let go of our attachments to our own preconceptions, God's ideas take over.

That is how we learn who we really are and where we live and move and have our being. That is the purpose of monastic spirituality.

Most of us suffer because we believe that we are what we are *not*. We are not our senses, thoughts, or feelings, though these things are certainly part of us. We are not even our personality, for the very concept of person *(persona)* is based on the role we play, like the mask used in the Greek theater. We are really something much deeper than any of these things. When we let go of the outer to discover the inner, then the inner can empower the outer. Once we discover this deeper self, then all the exterior aspects of who we are fall harmoniously into place.

All religions point to this way out. It is the way of letting go of our enslavement to the senses, emotions, and thoughts—through stillness, silence, and meditation—so that *God* can tell *us* what's what and who's who. It is through a death to the old self that a new person is born and functions in the freedom of God's plan. Eckhart Tolle, Deepak Chopra, and Wayne Dyer are popular self-help teachers who have tried to explain letting go of ego attachments and embracing the true self of God's Spirit in contemporary language. In fact, such reflections are as old as the question *Who am I?*

In Christianity this freedom happens most perfectly through understanding the bodily death of Jesus Christ and his rising from the dead. Our spirit too is reborn through the gift of God's Spirit. Then all of life becomes a miracle of rebirth and awakening in a way that cannot be achieved by anything in this material world. Christ is the perfect, and eternal, answer.

Experiences of body and mind come and go. But our deepest being, our spirit, remains forever. Our spirit sees beyond a wounded body, or a wounded soul, and intuits eternity in a moment; it knows all things in a flash. It is beyond all senses, emotions, and thoughts, but it builds on and empowers them all. Through pure spiritual intuition we can be present every-where even while here in space and time on earth. We can know all things without becoming a scholar or an intellectual. We can do all things while being fully aware of our human limitations and failings. We can know healing without seeking a cure. This is especially true when the Spirit of Christ aids us. This is the greatest discovery and deepest enlightenment for the inner hermit. "I can do all things through Christ who strengthens me!" (Phil 4:12).

When our inner hermit breaks through and is born again, it has a profound effect on the entire world. The world becomes our cloister, and we become instruments of peace and joy and, most especially, love. The Bible teaches that it only takes twelve enlightened people on the face of the earth to keep it from self-destructing. Jesus sent out twelve apostles. And there are more than twelve of us interested in cultivating our inner her-mit right now. We, too, all of us, are "whole and entire."

So let's look at some of the spiritual tools and traditions that will spark our spirit and enable us to make the world our cloister and bring God's peace and love to all the earth. We will learn how we can do this without ever leaving our home or neighborhood or country. What purpose in life could be more satisfying?

Silence and Stillness

⌇

More than anything, silence and stillness are the qualities that draw us to the hermit within and plant the seeds of the Spirit for us to bring peace to the world from wherever we are.

Knowing who we are, as well as who we are not, we understand the toll that human life can take on us. The mom with a full-time job is taking the children to school and is stuck in a traffic jam. The kids have gotten crazy in the back seat. The loudest one gets louder. The quiet one retreats into the private world of her iPod. This scene, or another like it, is familiar to any mother who is raising children.

This reminds me of Mary Chapin Carpenter's song "He Thinks He'll Keep Her." In that song the common scenario portrayed above is summarized in the phrase "She drives all day!" At the same time the song "Grey Street" by the Dave Matthews Band reflects the hearts of many women throughout the United States and other countries who feel that the whole world has gone almost irrevocably gray, even as they desperately long for a life of full color.

Men and women of every vocation often feel trapped in an endless circle of competition and the futility of trying to make a living in the West. By midlife they may have given up on ever reaching the goals they once felt within their reach. Depression sets in with little things at first. Then anger erupts and bitterness begins to poison every circumstance and relationship. Ultimately, they experience a deadly boredom with anything and everyone.

And then there are the overachievers. They thrive on activity and find energy in expending it. Most of my successful friends are like this, running flat out all the time. They rarely are melancholy; neither are they particularly reflective. Life is a constant cycle of exciting projects that are all consuming—until they move on to another one. I fear that one day it will all come crashing down on them as they awaken to the futility of it all. Then depression will come.

There is a better way.

At some point all of us begin to hear the faint but deep whisperings of the Spirit of God, calling us to something less that is in fact something much more. It is a call to silence and solitude, a journey into the deep heart of sacred stillness. In this call to solitude, silence, and stillness we discover the hermit within.

Usually, silence and solitude are joined together. One is not possible, or at least fruitful, without the other. For instance, if we seek both external and interior silence, we must establish an environment where this deep silence can be developed and can grow. That environment is solitude. When solitude and silence are joined together, they produce a sacred stillness that permeates every aspect of our life.

This way of stillness is based upon the example of Christ himself. Jesus first went to the desert to prepare for his ministry. He went to the place of the greatest stillness to prepare for the ultimate action. He went to the place of deafening silence to hear the most profound word. He went to the place where those of his day believed the demons dwelled in order to do battle with them. He went there to bring salvation and lasting peace to the entire world.

This way of stillness gave rise to the whole monastic and contemplative tradition in the Christian church. Those who wanted to follow Jesus more radically believed they needed to imitate his stillness before they could imitate his actions. They needed to understand his silence before they could speak his words. They needed to know his emptying of self through dying before they could proclaim the abundance of eternal life.

Most of us are not called to be a full-fledged monk or hermit. Most of us do not desire to live in actual monasteries or hermitages. Most of us live and work in cities or suburbs or as farmers in rural America. But there are steps all of us can take to help us establish the solitude and silence that give birth to an entire life of sacred stillness.

The most obvious steps involve time and space. We must provide an environment for interior silence and solitude by establishing some healthy exterior solitude and silence.

Most of us can take extra time each day by rising before the rest of the family, or by going to bed twenty or thirty minutes after the rest of the household has been tucked away. Practitioners tell us that if we have twenty to thirty minutes of uninterrupted meditation we will discover at least a moment of contemplation that will be enough to get us through much if not all of our day.

This practice covers time, but we also need to cover space. Most of us can find a prayer corner somewhere in the house. It can be a simple prayer corner with a crucifix or a sacred image of one of the saints and perhaps a candle or two. It is good to be able to sit or to kneel in such sacred places without having to shift around much. The less clutter the better. A simple prayer mat is sufficient.

At the beginning it might prove a bit difficult to carve this time and space out of our normal daily routine. But it can be done. We wouldn't cancel an important meeting with our boss, or a date with the romantic love of our life. If it is really important to us, then we keep the appointment even if we have lost our enthusiasm for it because we've had a rough day. Indeed, that's a great reason to do it. We do not give up when we

experience difficulty with ourselves or with our family in trying to make this part of our life. If we persevere, we will
discover that this practice and method bring great spiritual
refreshment.

But before we get too celebratory, we should also know
that the initial refreshment of such a practice may also take us
to deeper levels that sometimes can resemble dark nights of
the soul and indeed can be painful. But if we embrace these
dark nights, these periods of uncertainty and suffering, and
unite them with the dark night and suffering of our Savior,
Jesus Christ, we will emerge at the end of this process with
great light, great ecstasy, and great joy.

The way of stillness is no mere escape into illusion. In fact,
it is the way to the greatest confrontation of all—the confrontation with the darkness that lurks within our self-obsessed
hearts. This is personified in the deluded spirit we call the devil.
Though not self-obsessed, even Jesus had to confront temptation in the solitary deserts of Palestine. So did the early monks,
and all who followed after them. We have to confront these
demons within their own heart and soul. We are no exception.

Solitude and silence are wonderful refreshment, a healthy
alternative to the noise and chaos of this modern world. But
anyone who has spent more than just a few hours or days
practicing this knows that the process of rebirth from death to
self is often found only through some experience of travail.
Only then do we know the joys of the newborn child of the
Spirit of God.

Consider the analogy of the pond. The winds of this world
agitate the water. The winds are thoughts that stir up the waters of our soul so that they become muddy and unclear. Where
once they reflected an image of God, now they show shifting
shadows. All that remains is a distortion of the original image.

It is only when the waters settle that they become calm and
we can see our true image in them. Then we can reflect all life

around us and glimpse the very image of God. This is why it took Jesus forty days and nights of fasting and prayer in the Judean desert. This is why it takes most serious monks a lifetime. It will take years for us as well. But it can be done. If we are patient and sincere, God will find *us*.

As we continue this practice we begin also to see things at the bottom of the pond of our soul, which has become a collection place for all kinds of garbage thoughts and feelings. This trash has been tossed into our life over many years of unhealthy thought patterns. Slowly but surely all of this can be cleaned out, and the waters of our soul purified.

Sometimes it seems that as we get into the process of spiritual rebirth, all hell breaks loose. All the discarded and destructive stuff of our life comes to the surface. Our pond may seem downright ugly for a while. But this is just temporary. Compared to living in a continual state of agitation and fear, this is well worth the journey and easier than it looks if we but keep our eyes on the divine goal of peace in the mind of Jesus Christ.

So, then, will we take the time to enter into the tradition of sacred stillness for ourselves, or will we just read about it, and think about maybe doing it someday? The scriptures tell us that "today is the day of salvation. If today you hear his voice, harden not your hearts" (Ps 95:7–8; Heb 3:7–8). If we need rest from the burdens of this noisy and chaotic world, if we are tired of living in constant agitation, lack of clarity, and obsession, we come to the waters of life and still the waters of our soul. This is the way of Jesus. It is the way of the mystics and the saints. It can be our way as well.

Sacred Space

Sit in your cell as in paradise. Put the whole world behind you and forget it. Realize above all that you are in God's presence, and stand there with the attitude of one who stands before the emperor.

—FROM SAINT ROMUALD'S BRIEF RULE FOR HERMITS

We have spoken about how our body needs a space of prayer for us to be silent and still. This place is called a cell in monastic life, and the word is a wonderful symbol. Just as all cells in a body relate to and affect one another, all beings are connected to each other and to God. We learn this mystery in our private place of prayer, our cell. Paradoxically, it is in a cell that the entire world becomes our cloister.

When we think of a cell, we unfortunately tend to think of Alcatraz, or of "poor nuns" who have been locked away against their will, or of a secret cult where an autocratic leader does terrible things behind barbed-wire fences. But while some strange things have occasionally happened in monastic history, the hermit's cell has nothing to do with these popular folktales.

I can remember having such images when I was a boy. A group of us would often sneak onto the grounds of Ladywood, a forest around the Ladywood High School. Sisters operated it and lived there in a convent. Back then the school was only for girls, which made our adolescent hormones kick in. It was thrilling. We had heard that the nuns kept dogs to maul intruders like us if we emerged like wolves from the woods. Well, one day we snuck onto the grounds and came across a sister walking and praying her office. She smiled kindly at us and quietly continued her prayer walk. That was it. What a letdown! No fearful sisters, no dogs, and no girls! Plus no reprisals. In a sense this is similar to dealing with negative images of the cell, many of which are based on old folktales and prejudices. Real monasteries, convents, and hermitages are ordinary places with ordinary people.

The word *cell* is related to the word *celestial*. It is also the root of the word *cello*. It is supposed to be a place where heaven comes to earth. What a beautiful image, and one quite different from the popular understanding. Although we usually associate the word *cell* with a restriction, the root word is based on the concept of heaven coming to earth. It points to something beautiful and uplifting.

This word's meaning has some other paradoxical implications. First, it reminds us that the criminal prison system is meant to be a place for the reformation of life. It is not supposed to be only about confinement and punishment. Our understanding of prison falls far short of the original intention of the use of the word *cell*. No one is beyond redemption. Saint Paul was a murderer, as were some of the early monastic saints before they converted to Christ. After their reformation they became light for a world of darkness. A cell is a symbol for a place to ponder our life and see what is good and true.

The early system of dealing with lepers also coopted the word *cell*. Lepers not only lived in cells but, like monks, also wore the garb of a hermit, renounced the secular world, lived in quasi-monastic leprosarium communities in cells, and sometimes wandered as beggars from leprosarium to leprosarium.

Their commitment to this life was a sacred rite performed in a church before a bishop or priest. Lepers were considered special, consecrated, and holy. They could not interact with society because of the real or perceived risk of contagion, but they were not considered pariahs. The premise was that the lepers were a constant reminder to the rest of society to be compassionate and to care for the sick and homeless. The leper's cell, too, was a place of heavenly potential.

This has much to teach us today. All cells are related. Our place of prayer is connected to every other space on earth. What do we learn there, and how does it affect what we do when we leave our cell? How well do we care for our sick and infirm, who are extensions of ourselves? How well do we care for the aged in their cells? for the terminally ill? Cancer is the greatest killer in our midst. AIDS is often terminal. Both carry a stigma (from the word *stigmata*, meaning to bear the marks of the crucified Christ as Saint Francis did). If we get to the true meaning of some of these words, then we can see them as the blessing they really are.

A cell is meant to be a holy place, and one cell is a doorway to another. The word *cell* has a great personal meaning for those who desire to follow the call of the hermit within. The celestial aspect sees the cell as both a practical living space on earth and a heavenly place for prayer. As we've said earlier, it can be a designated room in a house or apartment or simply a small space with special meaning. It is a place where God can come to us. It is the place where we can learn what it means to make the world our cloister.

I have been graced by living in a hermit's cell most of my religious life, except for the times on the road ministering through music. For me, the cell has been a blessing but certainly has not always been easy. It has been a taste of heaven and a purgatory to prepare me for heaven. I always long for it while in ministry and do not really want to leave when I go out

for ministry. Yet it is sometimes a crucible beyond words. It
has reformed my very soul and made me aware of how far I
have yet to go.

At first the cell hides us for a brief time from the distractions
of the world. This is like paradise. It is rest and peace. But the
cell also brings us face to face with God and our personal self.
There is no place to hide. There are few distractions or diver-
sions. Yes, wise hermits allow for some simple recreation in
their cell, but it is limited in time and scope.

Hermits can become very creative in finding even small
things to distract them from God and the quest for truth and
reality. Things we would have thought trifles in the world now
become important to us. We can end up frittering our time
away as we fly from one thing to another all day without accomplishing anything of spiritual value. We can even use the-
ology or reading to distract us from the deeper work of simple
prayer and meditation before God. It is funny how we can use
the things of God to hide us from God when we are really
afraid to face God in solitude and silence.

When the futility of hiding behind such things is released,
we can begin facing God and ourselves in the crucible of deep
solitude and silence. It is there that we often discover how
much of our self-image, even our religious self-image, has been
an attempt to cling to our false self and ego triumphs. The
healing is in letting go.

Letting go is simple, but it is also difficult. It takes much
meditation and prayer. Breath after breath, prayer after prayer,
and year after year we approach some greater measure of
peace and insight. God's grace accomplishes this, but we set
the stage by taking time from our day to cultivate solitude and
silence in our cell.

Most of us do not live in a monastic cell, so the more extreme practices do not literally apply for us. But we can take
the spirit of such teachings and apply them to our secular life.

The hermit's cell in the Egyptian desert was a very simple affair. It was usually constructed with the help of hermit brothers in a single day. It was made of bricks and mortar resembling stucco made from the sands of the desert. The roof was made of reeds and palm branches.

Saint Antony of the Desert said that those who love the cell are like fish out of water when they are away from it. He also taught that overly strict solitude in the cell, and solitary life in general, is like pulling a bowstring too tight and for too long. Sooner or later it will break. In other words, too much of a good thing is not healthy for us. We need balance in all things.

Antony has another insight regarding prayer and work. One day he could not stay focused on prayer. His mind started to wander, and the more he tried to pray the worse the mental distractions became. He cried out to God to help him. At first God didn't seem to answer. Antony saw a monk praying and then getting up to do manual labor. The monk spent some quality time in each mode, prayer and work. Antony heard a voice that said, "Go and do likewise, and you shall be saved."

The moral to the story is that hermits need to pray undisturbed so prayer will energize work. And then they must use that energy in work. Balance is the key.

We can all learn what we need to know by sitting in the paradise of our cell. We will find right action in sitting still. We will learn, perhaps for the first time, what it means to pray.

Breath Prayer

We do it immediately when we are born. It is the last thing we do before we die. Breathing is the most basic requirement for human life. Uniting this gift of life with prayer is as natural as walking to church. That is one reason that most major religions use breathing as a device to help in prayer.

Breath prayer is a powerful tool for prayer. It is a springboard to mindfulness, meditation, and contemplation, which we will learn more about soon. It infuses and unites them. Many of us associate breath prayer exclusively with Eastern religions. But it is also a venerable ancient method used in Christian meditation. It has similarities to the Eastern methods on a physical and psychological level, but it has its own distinct Christian flavor and tone from a theological and mystical perspective.

The Hebrew words for Spirit mean "wind" and "intimate breath" (of God). It is also where we get our words *inspiration* and *respiration*. Jesus says that the Spirit of God is like the wind, and he breathes the Spirit upon the apostles for leadership before he ascends to heaven after his resurrection. The Spirit descends upon the whole assembly at Pentecost like a "strong, driving wind."

Because of these scriptural meanings, the monastic tradition of the Christian East found that uniting prayer with the breath helped in fulfilling Saint Paul's further admonition to "pray without ceasing" (1 Thes 5:17), since we must breathe to stay alive. Uniting prayer with the breath was also a way to

pray intuitively in the Spirit of God constantly, in a way beyond formal thought or emotion. Mystics found that uniting
the breath with the name of Jesus was a way to pray in the
name of Jesus intuitively, beyond concepts or words. This finally developed into the formal Jesus Prayer, which is united
with our breathing throughout the day.

In Hinduism, Buddhism, and Taoism, uniting meditation with
breath is fundamental. If we can control the most basic invol-
untary bodily function of life, then perhaps we can learn to
control the other senses and faculties that are voluntary. It is a
way to give the body and mind something to do without distracting it with too many complications. It also slows the body,
the emotions, and the thoughts in order to focus all of them
on the meditation at hand. Focusing on the breath is often the
beginning stage of meditation.

For the Christian, breath prayer is a way to do several things.
It unites us with Jesus in the Spirit of God. It slows the body so
that both thoughts and emotions are minimized and stabilized.
It gets us in touch with gospel poverty regarding the basic
thing we must do to physically be alive—breathe—and satis-
fies us with this ultimately simple act. Once the formal prayer
is learned and mastered, it teaches us to pray intuitively and
constantly with every breath.

With both Christian and non-Christian expressions some
bodily posture is recommended to enable the practitioner to
stay relatively still and quiet for an extended period of time,
say fifteen to thirty minutes.

How do we do it? How can we do it for even a minute, let
alone fifteen? We must first find a quiet place that is relatively
free from intrusion for the meditation time. Next, we sit either
in the traditional cross-legged position or in a straight-back
chair with our feet flat on the ground and head and shoulders
lined up as best we can to provide a stable and comfortable
pose.

Resting your hands in your lap to give them something to do that is minimal and relaxing. Imagine they are doves. Likewise, gently rest the tongue against the back of the front upper teeth on the upper palate. Keep your eyes slightly open, without focusing on any particular object, to stay awake and to keep from getting distracted by a particular object. Then breathe deeply from the diaphragm, or the navel.

This is the way we breathe at night when sleeping, and the way infants breathe constantly. It is also the way we singers are taught to breathe during singing. It relaxes the whole being yet brings the greatest amount of oxygen to the lungs and blood, making us alert and healthy. During most meditations we breathe gently and quietly through the nose.

We begin simply by remembering to breathe deeply, just as we did when we were born.

Next, we let everything go to God through Christ. We start with the body, emotions, and thoughts, and simply acknowledge how we are doing today with each. It may be positive or negative. We simply acknowledge whatever thought is there, and watch it go.

Then we recognize that these things of the senses, emotions, and thoughts are interdependent with creation in both immediate and far-reaching ways. This awakens us to the wonder of our being, to God's creation and incarnation, and generates an inner gratitude for all.

But we also recognize that, while these things are all part of our being, they are not our deepest and most essential being, for they are all transitory. Our bodies will pass away. Our emotions and thoughts rise and fall all the time. Even with the Christian belief in the resurrection of the body, we know that the resurrected body of Jesus was far more multidimensional than the limited and fragile bodies we now inhabit. Our bodies, emotions, and thought will be similar but radically changed and completed. Recognizing this, we let these things go and

die through the cross of Jesus. This enables us to let everything go in Christ.

When we practice this Christian breath prayer daily for a
few weeks, then months, and then years, we slowly find ourselves being reborn through the cross of Jesus Christ. It happens one day at a time, and one breath at a time. We become
more free from enslavement to the sensual appetites, the whirl-
wind of disordered emotions, and negative and confused
thoughts. We break through to the realm of our spirit in his
Spirit, and we see all of life as a miracle of rebirth, awakening,
and resurrection. Our inner hermit comes to life and brings us
peace in a whole new way of thinking, feeling, and perceiving
all of reality in God. When we know that, the whole world
benefits. The world has become cloister.

Many of us soon find ourselves praying the name of Jesus
with every breath. We are often surprised to find this a part of
the existing tradition of the church, and the monastic heritage.

One of the classical forms of Christian breath prayer is the
traditional Jesus Prayer of the monastic East. It is taught as
standard private prayer practice to novice monks on Mt. Athos
in Greece today. It has many similarities to the use of breath in
the meditation of the religions of the Far East, but, as the
monks are quick to point out, the similarities stop there. It
never loses its clear Christian focus.

The most ancient tradition of this prayer simply unites the
name of Jesus to each breath. This helped the monk to pray
in the name and Spirit of Jesus without ceasing, since one has
to breathe to stay alive.

Later, they added a formulated recitation to the prayer. They
first used the words, "Lord Jesus Christ, Son of God, have
mercy on me." Later still they added the words, "a sinner," to
the end for the sake of novice monks who needed more of an
emphasis on initial conversion.

"Lord Jesus Christ, Son of God, have mercy on me, a sinner."

Though the words are theologically replete with significance on the level of mind and emotion, the words are understood through pure spiritual intuition when prayed maturely. At first there is a need to get the actual significance of the words of the formula.

For those of us who speak English, *Lord* comes from the Old English that meant the feudal lord who could take the wheat of the farmers and turn it into bread. So, for us, it means the One who can turn our natural gifts and talents into spiritual nourishment.

Jesus comes from the Hebrew *Yeshua* or *Joshua* and means "salvation." In order to understand what it is to be saved, one has to have an appreciation of what it is to be lost and then rescued. Those who have gone through Twelve Step programs and had their lives literally saved from addiction and death have a good notion of the full meaning of the word.

Christ means "anointed." To be anointed by the Spirit means to live our lives more like the life of Jesus in our own day and time. A simple check of Saint Paul's wonderful list of the fruits of the spirit is a good way to discern this.

Son of God carries with it all the divine mysteries of the Trinity and the incarnation. Jesus is the eternally begotten Son of God within the Trinity for eternity. He is "God from God, Light from Light, True God from True God. Eternally begotten, not made. One in Being with the Father," as we recite in the Nicene Creed in most of our Christian churches. But it also implies all the mysteries of the incarnation. "For us, and for our salvation he came down from heaven, was born of the Virgin Mary, and became man," as the Creed says.

Have mercy on me is a phrase rich in meaning. Mercy is forgiveness plus deeply felt compassion. This is the love God has for us in Jesus Christ. No matter how badly we have sinned, or how far we have fallen, there is always a way back to God for those who want to return. This fills us with gratitude and love. It fills us with hope. Those who cry out for mercy know that their lives are in real need of a Savior. They are broken and humble and ready to ask for help in making a change for the better. Like the Prodigal Son they stumble back home to the Father, and the Father rushes out and meets them first.

A *sinner* was added for beginners. It is already implied in mercy. To sin means to miss the mark of perfection. The term was used in archery tournaments when the arrow missed the bull's eye. Most of us seek the things of God whether we know it or not. Most of us seek goodness and truth and beauty and love. But because we are still learning, we do not hit the bull's eye. Therefore our life is off center. It is out of balance. Like an out-of-balance tire on an Ozark mountain highway, if not corrected it becomes dangerous and life threatening.

These are just outlines of the full theological meaning of the Jesus Prayer. But to be properly understood, they must be understood mystically. Each time we breathe the Jesus prayer, we intuit its meaning. But it would actually be mentally confusing to try to grasp all of this with each breath and repetition. This would distract us from prayer. No, the full meaning of the Jesus Prayer is best grasped when intuited on the level of spirit *beyond* the senses, the emotions, and the mind. Then it can do the deeper work of salvation that will ultimately affect all the other areas for the better as well.

The Jesus Prayer is an ancient prayer tested by monastic tradition and time. It works well when used well.

There is also a way to pray the Jesus Prayer. We breathe in, "Lord, Jesus Christ, Son of God," and breathe out, "have mercy on me, a sinner." The first part is a filling prayer. The second part releases, lets go. With the in breath we allow ourselves to be filled with all that is good, holy, and true in the faith. In the second part we let go of the old patterns that stand in the way. I have found this second part most powerful in my own life.

Breathe, then.

Lord Jesus Christ, Son of God, have mercy on me, a sinner.

Mindfulness

One of the most helpful results of practicing stillness and learning to breathe is becoming aware of our senses, emotions,
and thoughts. Once we can relax in this stillness and simply
watch our thoughts, we open our soul to a greater awakening
of spirit. Eastern monks call this watchfulness. We call this
mindfulness.

There are many avenues to the hermit within and the higher
forms of prayer. I have taught the following exercise for years.

1. Sit in your meditation space. Breathe deeply to settle and
   still your senses, emotions and thoughts, and be aware of
   your spirit in the Spirit of God.
2. After breathing deeply, be aware of your body and the
   senses. Thank God for them as gifts from God. Be aware
   of the awesome wonder of their interconnectedness with
   the rest of creation, starting with your parents and family, and reaching out to the earth and all life that springs
   from it. Then, be aware that, despite the wonder of the
   body, it is only our temporary home during this lifetime.
   It will grow old, degenerate, and die. It will decompose in
   the grave. It will then be resurrected in a new and more
   wonderful form. Also be aware that in this fallen world
   the disordered sensual self is sometimes a cause of great
   trouble and pain to the soul. So we bring the body, and
   all that it is, to the cross of Christ and let it go. By doing
   this, all that is dysfunctional and out of order on our

physical level more naturally finds its place in the will of God, and we know peace. We know the first fruits of resurrection and new life even in this temporary bodily home.

3. Next, move to the emotions. Go through the same steps as with the senses. Be aware of the gift from God the emotions are, and thank God for them. Know that they are interdependent and conditioned by the other things of this phenomenal world. If we experience pleasure we are excited and happy. If things do not go as we want, we are agitated and unhappy. Know that these feelings are also temporary and impermanent. As conditions change, so do our emotions. They come and go, rise and fall, with the shifting conditions in our life. They are part of us but they are not the deepest being of who we really are. So we can relax and peacefully let them go at the cross of Jesus. This brings greater peace and gratitude as we surrender our experiences to God.

4. Next come your thoughts. Unless they are God's thoughts, these can be killers of joy. So, as with senses and emotions, first become aware of the thoughts that are passing through your mind without judgment. Observe that some are negative and some are positive, some clear, others unfocused. All of them are about the past or the future. Thank God for the gift of *God's* thoughts and for your spiritual mind. Realize that thoughts come and go. We have thoughts, but we are not our thoughts. Our real Self is filled with God's thoughts. So we bring all of our thoughts to the Christ and surrender them to him. We pray, "God, let me know only your thoughts." As you do this, you can sense your thoughts draining away, along with the tension and stress they often cause. For a moment you are in the present and know "the peace of Christ which passes all understanding" (Phil 4:7).

5. Now, having let go of the senses, emotions, and thoughts that separate you from the love of God, become aware of your spirit in God's Spirit, essence to Essence, breath to Breath. Breathe in this wonderful union with the deepest Essence beyond all thoughts, emotions, and sensual perceptions, yet building and empowering them all. Take some unhurried time to simply *be*. Breathe the awakening of your spirit in the Spirit of God.
6. After some quality time in the place of spirit, get up and go about the rest of your day, having first thanked God for any graces received.

Using the above skills we can begin to apply this mindfulness to daily activity. Taoists say that we refine the breathing of the body to cultivate the *chi* (energy), and refine the *chi* to allow the emergence of spirit, or *shen*. Practices such as Tai Chi allow this refinement to work from the outside in, so to speak, and then from the inside out.

Christians say that the asceticism and discipline of the senses of the body and the passions and thoughts of the soul lead us to rediscover our spirit in God's Spirit. This is a journey from the energies of body and soul to our spiritual essence. Once we break through and become aware of this we are reborn, and our thoughts, emotions, and senses are refined. This is because we have reset the priorities of our whole life. We also move from the outside in, and then work back from the inside out.

When this happens we begin to reassess everything we do in life. We begin to question why we worry about what people are thinking of us. We begin to observe ourselves eating, drinking, speaking, and working, and we are grateful. Even a toothbrush has life. Mindfulness is a practice that revolutionizes our whole world. It radically reduces the time we waste on our ego-centered guilt, worry, and anxiety over the past and future. Practically, this often means less time in front of the TV or computer, less time eating and drinking out of frustration and desire for comfort, less time gossiping or speaking in order to stroke our ego. It also means less time working for mere external satisfaction or looking for ego gratification.

At first this discipline seems impossible to achieve. It is indeed difficult to be mindful every moment. We can't easily change deeply entrenched patterns of thought. But we can choose to practice mindfulness, aware that even a little bit of mindfulness goes a long, long way.

As in Tai Chi, mindful Christians begin to flow in all areas of life. Life becomes graceful and filled with ease even in difficult situations.

All of this involves the development of spiritual skill. But we have special grace to practice it. Jesus is the great spiritual master who releases his followers from having to bear the impossible burden of finding such spiritual greatness themselves. It is his grace that lets us discover it. The saints and their various teachings on active and contemplative prayer witness to an entire heritage of such greatness.

Western Christian tradition speaks of the purgative, illuminative, and unitive ways to God. In other words, first we experience suffering in shedding the threads of our ego, then we get insight, and finally we realize, if only for a moment at first, our oneness with God. We begin to know that "nothing can separate us from the love of God" (Rom 8:38).

Nothing is more awesome.

Taming the Monkey Mind

*If your mind wanders . . . don't give up
but hurry back and try again.*

—Saint Romuald, founder of the Camaldolese

We start off with the best intentions. We sit right, breathe right, and focus our mind. Then our mind begins to wander every which way, except the way we would like it to go. What do we do with a wandering mind?

The Hindus call it the monkey mind. Thoughts jump from one tree to the next, one bar of the cage to the other, with no purpose known to anyone but the monkey. This agitated state makes it impossible to focus on any one thing. Meditation settles the monkey down; our thoughts become a bit clearer.

We all want to have a method that works quickly and neatly. But we must practice, practice, practice, in peace and tranquility. We need to bring the mind gently back to the focus of the meditation, to do it over and over without getting frustrated, obsessed, or manic in the process. Meditation masters, teachers, and students have experienced this for millennia.

There are pointers that some have found helpful. The mystical classic *The Cloud of Unknowing* uses a simple mental tool to fight off unruly thoughts: picture your wandering thoughts as small rocks coming at you. Slow down their progress by visualizing the approaching stones coming in slow motion. As they get close, simply move your head gently to one side or the other and let them pass by harmlessly. Most folks find that this little mental device actually works well.

Francis of Assisi once molded a clay pot. He was pleased with how it turned out. During prayer and meditation he couldn't get the image of the pot out of his mind. The more he tried, the harder it was to let it go. So he went out after prayer and smashed the pot. This is a bit more aggressive response than I would recommend. Sometimes such extreme measures actually make the image stronger by putting too much energy into it—like putting fuel on a fire. But there *are* times when the distracting thought is so entrenched that something more radical must be tried. But you get the point—distractions distract. They come. They are unavoidable. You have to be patient in overcoming them, even if you never do so for more than a little while. That's a lot, and good for you!

The statement quoted in the chapter opening from Saint Romuald, who lived in the tenth century, is wise, simple, and profound: "Don't give up but hurry back and try again." This says it all. Most of us give up meditation after a very short time. Romuald has a cure for that: persevere. There is a gentle tone to his simple answer. Too much effort can inadvertently wake old passions. As the monk Evagrius warns, "Do not turn the cure of a passion into a passion." He knew that we can only work with this process a step at a time, and that trying to force these things will lead nowhere.

For example, in the time of the charismatic renewal we often saw the same people come through the prayer line over and over again. What they were looking for was a "big bang" from God. An occasional experience like that is not a bad thing. But if we think that is the aim of prayer, then we get ourselves into all kinds of spiritual trouble. Passion is helpful, especially at the beginning of our conversion. But as we begin to develop and mature, our prayer and meditation patterns also change and mature.

The best advice I can give is to bring your mind simply and gently back from its distraction by focusing on the theme of your meditation. And when your focus disappears again in a second or in twenty seconds or in a minute, do it again. Do it one or a thousand times. Do it from now until the end of time. Do not worry that you do it repeatedly. This is normal. If done gently, your mind will come back on its own through God's grace. Even if only for a moment, that is enough.

I remember a Christian song about going to a monastery door to ask what they did there all the time. The porter answered, "We fall down, and we get up." As the inquirer walked away, he realized that is true for anyone seeking God. We all fall down. It is not falling down that is the issue. What is at issue is whether or not we get back up.

And so it goes with breath prayer or mindfulness or meditation. We fall down, and we get up! That is perfection.

Christian Meditation
and Contemplation

~~

Meditation is an esoteric word to some of my born-again Christian friends. But many are now seeking something deeper than their initial experiences of new life in Christ. They want to mature. They seek deeper waters.

Many of those searching for solitude, silence, and stillness are not really sure what they are searching for. They only know that the traditional church structures they were raised with do not cut it anymore. Perhaps this is because we only see the deeper things of faith by having the faith to see *spiritually*. Once we go through some kind of awakening, we discover it was there all along. Christianity carries a huge contemplative tradition for anyone who is searching. Regrettably, we have not been very skilled at putting out the welcome mat to those seekers.

Meditation is part of the ancient Christian heritage of contemplative prayer. Scripture says, "Meditate on the law of the Lord day and night" (Ps 1:2). Jesus spent long hours in solitary meditation and prayer. He was a master of the connection between mindfulness and the rest of our spiritual life. Saint Paul also teaches that the spiritual renewal of the mind is intimately connected with the quality of our entire spiritual life (Rom 12:2).

"As a man thinketh in his heart, so he is" (Prov 23:7).

So what is Christian meditation? Is it different from contemplation? These two ideas sometimes get confused and have been used in different ways throughout history.

Greek philosophers long before Christ defined *meditation* as a state of spiritual intuition beyond thought or emotion. Eastern religions also mean this when they speak of meditation (or *samadhi*). *Contemplation* has generally meant to reflect on or mull over something in a way that involves the mind and the emotions.

But in the Christian West we mean the *exact opposite* of these usages. For us, *meditation* means to reflect on or consider or turn over in our minds a spiritual truth. By *contemplation* we mean spiritual intuition beyond thought or emotion.

For us in the West, meditation is pondering the things of God with our mind and heart, considering what is knowable of God and his creation through our normal ways of perception. Contemplation is going beyond our thoughts or emotions into a pure union of our spirit in the Spirit of God.

Contemplation is a gift of God beyond our perception. We don't go to it, it comes to us. It is pure union of being in Being. As God is simply I AM, so we simply ARE in him when experiencing contemplation. Contemplation happens when we stop thinking of God, and God's idea takes over!

Since early times in the Christian West meditation has been part of a process of prayer that leads to contemplation and to mystical union with God. The monastic tradition teaches sacred reading, vocal prayer, meditation, and contemplation. It begins with reading a sacred text in a prayerful way. This is not like doing a bible study. It may only involve a short passage or a sentence from the sacred text. The source may be scripture or the writings of a master or saint. The text is taken into the soul, and we think about it. As Mary did, we "ponder these things in our heart" (Lk 2:19).

From reading, we effortlessly pass over into meditation. We use our mind to stir our imagination and our emotions. We visualize the events of the text. We experience the text on an emotional level as we relive the life of Christ or a saint or the personalization of their teachings through promptings of the Spirit. We seem to experience the visualization as we are transported back to the Palestine of Christ or the era of a saint. Often I was sure that I could feel the sands of the Middle Eastern deserts between my toes! This all is God's way of getting our whole being involved in the process of conversion, or turning back to God through Christ.

It is interesting that the ancients actually recited a text aloud even when they read in private. This slows our reading down. *Vocal prayer* is also a venerable part of the tradition. When we take the time to speak or even mouth the words of the text, we minimize the temptation to speed through the word of God. We maximize the opportunity to meditate.

The most helpful text to the monastic is the psalms. "The path you follow is in the psalms," said Saint Romuald. "Don't leave it."

Many monks as well as associates have a hard time getting into the psalms. They seem boring. One of the most venerable women in our community once said, "I believe in Jesus and the New Testament, but I don't think God wrote the Old Testament!" I was surprised, but now after many years I understand where she was coming from.

Many Christians read the Hebrew scriptures and see only an angry, tribal God. Great love infuses the Old Testament, but it also has a lot of blood, brutality, and fear. A lot of "My God is bigger than your God" is in it too. It isn't until Christians read the New Testament and the Gospel of Jesus that their hearts turn toward a more consistently compassionate God. They believe it is a more complete revelation.

For Christians, the New Testament builds on the Hebrew scriptures and completes it with forgiveness and redemption. And the church continues to build upon tradition. About every one hundred years Catholics need another ecumenical council or synod to clarify truths for Christian living. Every few years monks and nuns need a general chapter. We are all called to preserve what is good from the past but also to build upon and go beyond it.

Here in the Ozark Mountains we have gotten pretty good at building rock walls. You first need a good foundation and cornerstone. Once you start building, you need to set the next stone right on top of the older ones. If you let the wall lean to the right or the left, it will collapse. The same is true with preserving and building upon the old. We must sit clearly on what has come before. But we must go into space that has never been occupied by a stone before.

The psalms are proven steppingstones. The word *psalm* comes from the Hebrew word meaning "praises" and from the Greek for "songs played on a harp." There are 150 songs of praise in the Book of Psalms. From the beginning of Christianity monks and others have prayed or sung the psalms from a book called a Psalter, and later the Breviary or Divine Office. At mass, Catholics sing or pray a psalm after the first scripture reading. Perhaps the most popular is Psalm 23, "The Lord Is My Shepherd."

The psalms express some of the most comforting and joyful parts of the scriptures. They also express pain. These things are real parts of our life with God and others. I like them because they express the wide array of human emotions and thoughts in response to God's calling upon our life. I believe they were kept so prominently in communal Christian worship because they represent a most honest and human response to following God in the Old and New Testaments.

But often at mass when we hear the responsorial psalm we don't really listen to it because we are stuck on the style of the music or the lack of interest in the lector or non-participation in those around us. We need to get over that. And we do that through understanding and practice and sincerity of heart.

Saint Romuald said, "Take every chance you can find to sing the psalms in your heart and to understand them with your head."

This is beautiful. It hits the nail right on the head. So often we think that getting the right liturgical form or professional performance can solve our problems. We think that we can call in a good exterminator to fix our liturgical termites! But that is too simple and too superficial.

If we simply start praying with sincerity, spiritual intuition, the prompting of the heart and the understanding of the mind, then how polished the choir is at mass no longer becomes a hindrance to our experience of Jesus. Don't get me wrong. I believe we need good musicians, lectors, pastors, and all the rest. But I also believe that the external qualities of worship are not the gauge to determine the spirituality of a monastic house or parish. The ushers might not smile much, the musicians may be off key, and the preaching pedestrian. But nobody's perfect.

The real thing is to *pray*, and to do so without judgment of the monastery or parish, the leaders or participants. There will always be enough to complain about. We must move beyond this if we are to express love, joy, and peace. If we can pray where we are, be friendly ourselves, and be ready to volunteer when asked, things begin to improve for everyone. The hermit within asks no less.

Saint Francis wrote: "Say the Office devoutly, not concentrating on the melody of the chant, but being careful that their hearts are in harmony so that their words are in harmony with their hearts, and their hearts are in harmony with God. This aim should be to please God by purity of their heart, not to soothe the ears of the congregation by their sweet singing."

So performance is not the issue. Personal likes and dislikes are not the issue. The issue is to pray well so that others can be led back into prayer.

So learn more about the psalms. Read good books about them. Read from the Book of Psalms itself in the Hebrew scriptures.

Monks pray or sing the Divine Office every day. It is a singular source of spiritual enrichment. Saying the psalms is just as helpful as singing them. Inner hermits, too, will find nourishment and inspiration from making the psalms a regular part of their life. But this is only the beginning stages.

As you find yourself moving forward from breath prayer to mindfulness to meditation, you soon recognize another change. Occasionally, and then more regularly, you are almost effortlessly transported into a contemplation that is beyond thoughts, emotions, images, forms, or words. This is the place of pure spiritual intuition. Here you know oneness with the ultimate Being. Your body and soul have been used to ramp you over to pure experience of the Spirit of God. This process includes senses, emotions, and thoughts, sure, but it completely transcends them all in a way that fulfills everything.

You come to know it is true that "in God we live and move and have our being" (Acts 17:28).

When Necessary, Use Words

The practice of prayer in a place of sacred stillness is a healing gift. Its energy moves out and touches everyone. The world is our cloister from the spot where we are sitting. But when we finish our set period of silence and prayer, we too must go out in the world, and we must be "spoken."

We often regret conversations in which we speak too much. We talk too much when we are nervous or insecure or unsure of ourselves. We talk to cover the fact that we don't feel confident in what we're talking about or are afraid to share our authentic self with others. This is ironic. We talk too much when we don't have much to say! We talk about superficial things because we don't want to share the depths of our soul with others.

Scripture tells us that those who are wise say little but communicate much. Those who talk too much often relay little.

We experience this phenomenon in a new way through the Internet. This medium can be a great blessing. But it is sometimes used for messaging and emailing too much while communicating very little. The Internet makes the wisdom of the ages available with the click of a mouse or the tapping of a touch pad. But with all this knowledge available, few actually learn wisdom. With all these words, we don't communicate.

Christian silence makes for better "speech," for better communication. It is a tool to help us *listen,* really to hear others. Then we can truly listen to God and speak with a wisdom that helps others instead of simply making ourselves feel important. Words born of silence say only what others really need to hear. The other talk is born of a pride and insecurity that have yet to surrender the false self to godly silence.

Christian hermits don't see silence as a virtue in itself. It is important only as a means to understanding the incarnate Word. This Word is not a dogma or legislation or a sentence found on the pages of a spiritual book. Jesus is Word even in his silence. We need to share his silence to know him.

Many of us are bombarded with words all day. At work we are besieged with the competition mentality, both from our coworkers and those from other organizations that compete with us. To call this a high-stress environment is an understatement. On the home front we hear the sounds of kids playing or fighting, the television turned up too loud and for too long. As parents, we frequently end up coiling up into an emotional fetal position so that we can just shut things out.

Out of my own studies of what constitutes wisdom in the scriptures, I have realized that the wise are those who are always prepared to be silent and to listen. Then they have the authority to speak. The wise speak seldom, but when they do speak, their word is powerful, healing, and peaceful. It is better to spend our time listening in meditation and contemplation, so that when we do speak, we have something worth saying. Jesus retired into deserted places to pray and only then came out to teach.

There are different kinds of silence. Prayerful silence helps us to store up wisdom and teaches us to become good listeners. Foolish silence simply means thinking we have nothing to say about anything. Then there is the cruelest silence of all, the silence of those who have given up and are turned in upon themselves after years of being hurt, belittled, or put down. Last, there is the silence of those who dare not speak but judge everyone and everything under the cover of silence. This silence is ugly and breeds a spirit of negativity that can infect others even without words.

When we first experience spiritual silence we feel as if we're dipping ourselves into a life-giving bath of grace. For most of us it is the first time we have been able to "let go" and experience the grace and presence of God. Later, silence and solitude can lead us into a place where all of our ego illusions are brought to life and peeled back like the layers of an onion. This can be tough. But it ultimately leads to even greater grace.

One of the greatest tests of our silence is how well we listen. The most obvious place to begin is with listening to others. And the greatest test for this is to see how soon we begin to conceptualize our response as the other person speaks. We do not want to be scrupulous about this, but if we find ourselves formulating our answers before we hear the comments or questions of others, then we can be pretty sure that we do not have a silent soul.

But there is even more to a life of listening. Listening to people is just the beginning. If we truly begin to live this life of listening we will find ourselves, like Saint Francis, listening to the creatures with which we share Planet Earth. We will also listen to the creation all around us, sentient and non-sentient. They all have messages from God—if we have the ears to hear. It is not easy to abuse these forms of life for our own profit if we are engaged in a life of listening.

This lesson also applies to our life in the church. If we become good listeners we hear what the church says to us in both the mystical and pragmatic ways. We truly listen to what the pope, the bishops, and the pastors of our parish churches have to say. When we disagree with them, we try to look more deeply into their hearts as human beings who have dedicated their lives to Jesus just as we have done. And they will respond the same to us. That common call will never allow us to become enemies. We all must learn how to listen to every brother and sister in the church, as children of one God created in his image. Then life becomes a complete miracle and mystery in Christ. It's really not that hard. All we need is love.

The person who inspired me most on this topic was a Franciscan friar, Alan McCoy. He said that many times he was sent on Vatican delegations to troubled areas of the world. The delegation would then report to the Vatican personally. Sometimes it reached conclusions contrary to the party line. Fr. Alan told us that though these meetings could have been tense, he never forgot how much the various cardinals and bishops to whom they reported wanted to serve Jesus, the church, and all people everywhere. When he focused on their unity in these things, it made their differences cordial and infused with love and respect. How different this is compared to the tense and combative meetings among potential enemies or rivals. How can we reach peace if we do not first have peace in our deepest heart and soul?

Sacred silence is both external and internal. Externally, we establish times and places for silence, perhaps our prayer corner or prayer room at a specific time. For some, silence is good first thing in the morning for twenty minutes or so. Others might find it easier in the evening after the day winds down. Either way, please do not say that it cannot be done. The many families who have practiced silence successfully prove this untrue; it is a welcome part of their daily schedules. Coupled with traditional prayers, these times can be a great time of bonding.

External silence provides the environment for interior silence. Most folks who stick to this schedule discover a slight element of peace coming into other aspects of their lives initially. Silence then permeates inward and then flows back out of the soul into all areas of our lives. Even in the midst of the busyness of business or family life we begin to find peace.

The sacred character of words is best discovered when one spends time in silence. Then, from silence, words begin to take on a whole new power to bring healing and love.

Solitude and Community

⁓

By now we are beginning to understand this whole thing about solitude, silence, and sacred stillness. Even our daily work and rounds in the secular world are becoming easier. Work and family still bring people problems, but we are learning to listen and deal only with real issues. Instead of just hammering away with our ideas of what is good and what is bad and with little or no understanding, we can now bring peace to others because we have found greater peace in our own soul. Even monks in monasteries experience their own version of this scenario within the normal activity of monastic life and the reception of new members. Younger monks might now be numerically older, with vocations coming later in life, but in the monastery they are still young in community time and usually have much to learn. They are monastic kids, so to speak. As monks mature they begin to find peace through the ebb and flow of monastic life.

Be that as it may, and as normal as family and community are, we sometimes find ourselves feeling lonely in the midst of typical American life. We may be in the midst of tens of thousands of people on the freeway, but we still find ourselves feeling lonely and scared. Even in monasteries we often find ourselves feeling very alone even though we are living in intense intentional community with others. Yet from this paradox we may find the deeper spiritual truths of God.

The solution for this loneliness is authentic community. Odd as it may sound, hermits have needed the support of like-minded people in a community of peers since the very beginning. Historically, this has been lived out in various ways. In the deserts of Egypt, Palestine, and Syria, it meant living in a cell as far as ten miles away from a common center where the hermits would meet once a week for a gathering prayer and shared feast on Saturday evening and a celebration of the mass on Sunday. From there the monks would gather supplies and go back out to their cells, where they would more effectively spend the entire week in prayer.

Saint Benedict of Nursia (480–547), who is considered the father of Western monasticism, began his monastic life by living as a hermit in a cave for three years. The solitude was so intense that a priest had to come and remind him to celebrate Easter with him. But in his rule, Saint Benedict describes a cenobitic or community-oriented monasticism as the safest way for the average monk. Yet he still reserves the highest honor for the hermits, who first lived in the midst of the community for many years and after this went forth into strict solitude.

The tenth and eleventh centuries witnessed many radical reforms to return to the way of the hermit without jeopardizing or belittling monastic cenobitism. This way is called semi-eremitism. Some of the great socio-hermits are Saint Romuald, the founder of what we today call the Camaldolese, and Saint Bruno, the founder of the Carthusians. Both of these saints brought the average semi-eremitical monk into a combined experience of the hermitage and the cenobium, solitude and communion. This involved hermits spending great times of prayer within their own cell. But three or so times a day the monks met in the chapel for the monastic office. Also, they met daily or weekly for a meal together, and there would be time for weekly or monthly recreation as they walked the hills together and talked of spiritual things. At Little Portion Hermitage we have one recreation day a week. We go to town or the nearby lake, or we watch quality DVDs. Or we just take a walk in the woods. We do this alone or together.

What does this say to us? I believe it means that very few hermits are able to live with virtually no human contact with the church or the world. Those who do are usually called recluses. They still celebrate the monastic office and receive the sacraments of the church, but they do this in strict solitude. Such people are hard to find. There are many others called to the semi-eremitical way of life; they hunger and thirst for solitude and silence, but they need human contact as well. They might go to church on a daily basis to sing the monastic office with others or to celebrate the mass with community. Though I give concerts around the country to teach the word of God and heighten awareness of the needs of the poor and of refugees, I am one of those drawn to this kind of life.

This kind of solitude is not usually viable for those who live in the secular world and seek to discover and nourish the hermit within themselves. They have not only the option but also the obligation to spend quality time with their families and with their coworkers. But discovering that inner hermit, and expressing it in their own way, is what makes them leaven in the world.

So how does semi-eremitism apply to you? In more ways than you might think.

On a weekly basis you might go to church only on Sundays and holy days. At the very most you might have one other day or evening dedicated to the work of the church. But all through the rest of the week you choose to find your own rhythm between solitude and communion in the family and the work place. You learn this from studying, praying, and practicing. You cultivate the hermit within. You meditate. You cultivate awareness of your relationship to God and all creation. You trust that you cannot go wrong. Your inner voice is the voice of the Holy Spirit.

No matter what form of eremitism works for you, there is a teaching from Evagrius Ponticus, an ascetical writer from the fourth-century deserts of Christian Egypt, that works for all of us. He says that the hermit is the one "separated from all, but united to all." This clearly speaks to our mystical union with God and communion with every other child of God, and that means everyone. Real solitude unites us with all humanity, all sentient life, and all creation. It does not separate us. Yes, we sometimes have to set boundaries in order to protect our solitude, but we don't do it out of callousness or lack of love. Indeed, the opposite is true. The more we go into authentic solitude to set the environment for mystical union with God, the more we are in communion with every person on earth, believer and unbeliever, past, present, or future, beginning with the household of faith.

The inner hermit needs solitude. But the inner hermit also needs community. It makes us better hermits, better Christians, better family members and celibates, and better human beings.

The Active
and Contemplative Life

We in the West have a hard time being still. Attention Deficit Disorder (ADD) is one of the epidemic diseases of our time. One cause is a chemical imbalance in the brain that makes us unable to sit still and concentrate or focus on one thing for any length of time. It is also caused by allowing an environment of hyperactivity to snowball through most of our lives and culture. It affects not only children but also adults. It is difficult for most of us to sit still. It is hard for us to just "be" with the One Who Is. We are constantly working on a new project, setting new goals, and accomplishing bigger and better things. While some of this comes from the entrepreneurial spirit that helped to make our nation great, most of us will readily admit that it has gotten way out of control.

It takes a long time to understand and appreciate what stillness is all about. This is true of monks, nuns, and sisters as well as laypersons. It is true for most aspiring inner hermits as well. Most of us know how to pray actively for things that come from our thoughts, emotions, and senses. We know how to pray at church, even with the activity there. We even know how to pray in the car or at the office or on the job site. But finding a place of real stillness is difficult for most of us. How many of us get to be completely still for twenty to thirty minutes a day? Dream on. But don't give up those dreams just yet!

The ancient Christian tradition appreciated sacred stillness *(heschyia)*. Early Christians considered it a great and necessary gift from God to lead us on to deeper spirituality. It begins with stilling the body, then the thoughts and emotions, and finally leads to the greatest gift of all: contemplation.

Contemplation appears as a grace in our lives after we have seriously engaged in the practice of solitude and silence, stilling our body and our soul for some time. Only occasionally does it happen quickly. But it does happen, so we do not give up. Usually we experience some initial graces after only a few weeks, but they are initial and sometimes even fleeting. They are meant to encourage us to keep going and to keep faith once the tougher work begins. The deeper stuff takes months and years. But anyone who has experienced it will tell you that it is well worth the wait.

Before inner stillness is given to us as a grace of God, most of us have to do the preliminary work to get ready for this most gracious encounter. An example might help here.

As an itinerant minister, I have become especially aware of the hard work done by others before I arrive for dinner. All I do is show up, but others have to do a lot of work to get the dinner ready.

Contemplation is like Jesus coming to dinner with us. Before he joins us we have to do all kinds of preparations. We clean the house or room where the dinner will be. Then we get the food started. Often it takes a good cook hours to prepare the meal. Last, we set the table. But we cannot get started until Jesus, the guest of honor, shows up. While there is a general time for supper, Jesus is known for surprising his hosts as to the precise time he arrives. This is due to his taking all the time necessary with each stop along the way. So we must learn to be patient. Once Jesus arrives, his presence fills us with joy. We are happy. And we have a wonderful meal with him. We almost forget all the hard work that went into getting the meal ready, or the work yet to do in cleaning everything up. Such is the euphoria of communion and true contemplation.

I have also been part of the hosting community during a visit of our local bishop to our hermitage after a fire we had on April 28, 2008. He was to make a pastoral stop in conjunction with some other stops in our vicinity. There was a time set for the visit. But he was late. Thirty minutes became one hour, then an hour and a half, and then two hours. Some of us were getting nervous. But as soon as the bishop arrived, there was nothing but grace and love shared mutually between our community and him and his visiting priests. In the end he took far more time with us than was scheduled.

This is also the case with those living from our inner hermits. We have to do the work of salvation to get ready for the coming of Jesus into our daily lives. But Jesus is free to show up in a way that can surprise us.

All of these activities in preparation for the coming of the Spirit into our lives are considered the "active life" in classical monastic spirituality. They are things that we can do either physically or mentally. They also calm and redirect the emotions. They are important, but not as important as the next stage. This is the stage of the contemplative life where pure union with God is experienced. This is the goal of everything in the active life.

Only after being rooted in such tried and tested things does one begin to get glimpses of the real goal: contemplative life. This life builds on, but is beyond, the stages or tools of the active life. It is beyond all works or meditations, but it builds on them all and further enlivens them all. When the contemplative life is truly discovered, then the power of the Spirit emanates back out through the things of the active life to keep us grounded and to reach out to help others making this journey. The world becomes our cloister when we go out into the world and bring the fruits of the Spirit with us, without ever having to say a word.

For the average inner hermit one of the active things that is enlivened is family life. The way of the inner hermit is not an escape from appropriate relationships with family and friends. Most especially, it is not a way to duck out of legitimate duties to family and society. When rightly practiced, the way of the inner hermit makes one a better participant in any social family, community, or group. The same is true for the monk or sister in a monastery or religious community, which becomes their primary family.

Once we have stilled the bodily senses and our emotions and thoughts through solitude and prayer, the spirit emerges in contemplative union with God and communion with all creation. This is when a state of contemplative watchfulness begins to pervade everything in our life and God is active even when we are standing still.

Once we have learned mindfulness, we can more easily turn ourselves over to the energy of God's thoughts. An example of this is the Eastern monk's analogy taken from the spider. The spider weaves its web and then waits in complete stillness. Only from this stillness can it feel even the slightest movement of the web as a small prey flies into it and gets entangled. Likewise for the inner hermit, stilling body and soul so that the still and serene spirit might emerge is of paramount importance. Then we can rightly discern whether the thoughts that come to us are ours or from God.

But this mindfulness, or watchfulness, is not paranoia or scrupulosity. Scrupulosity is like a pebble in one's shoe. A pebble can keep us from walking well, and from running altogether. Sometimes the best way for the devil to defeat us is to get us so paranoid about evil that we become afraid to do much at all, or we become anxious and judgmental of everything and everyone. Real watchfulness comes when we let go of our old sensual, mental, and emotional patterns. God comes to us with peace and calm.

Do you wish to be an active presence for God's good in the world?

Then "be still," the Psalmist says, "and know that I AM God."

The Music of God

The active contemplative begins to hear the music of God in the midst of the world. The sounds we hear through the media are often only noise. Today we find ourselves bombarded with a music born of a culture of confusion. It takes courage and perseverance to break through from the audio clutter of our society to the deeper music of God and humanity. This clarity comes through controlling our senses, emotions, and thoughts through asceticism, meditation, and contemplation that clears out the noise in our spirit and soul.

Once we begin to clear out the clamor, we begin to hear more truthfully. But what do we hear? As a musician, I have studied several treatises that say God created with music. But not the simple music we hear with our ears. It is the music of the spirit and soul.

God is perfect spiritual music. The analogy of a well-tuned harp was used by the early church fathers to describe the unity of the church. But the music they speak of is no mere earthly song. It is profoundly spiritual and mystical.

In scripture we learn much from the creation accounts of Genesis and John's Gospel. Here God creates through the Spirit in the Word, followed by light, and then form. All else flows from this. A pattern of spirit and sound, light and form, permeates the creation accounts of scripture. This music is the perfect harmony of various waves of created energy in sound, light, and form, all animated by God's creative Word. It is a symphony of God's Spirit.

In human beings sound and light are waves of energy perceived by the ears and eyes. Even solid physical objects are waves of energy, vibrating at various speeds to create a solid form perceptible to the touch. All of creation is the music of energy waves moving in perfect harmony, proportion, and rhythm.

Interestingly, modern physics speculates about a "theory of everything," in which scientists propose that the smallest things in creation are "strings" that pulsate at different rates, creating a kind of "music" that holds all the universe together. Furthermore, they propose, there may be as many as eleven different dimensions of reality besides our own. Thus, there is much, much more going on all around us than we can perceive with the faculties of the bodily senses, let alone the mind and emotions. These things can only be known through the pure intuition of the spirit.

The mystics say that in the mystical state we can see sound and hear color. There is more to us than appears at first glance. We have powers we barely perceive. I believe that this was our original mode, and will be again when we begin to live in eternity.

This harmonious music is part of God's very being. And, says Saint Paul, "it is in God that we live and move and have our being." We are notes in God's perfect harmony of goodness and selfless love. This awesome balance and peaceful harmony is perfectly manifested in the Trinity of Father, Son, and Holy Spirit. It is perfect logic, but beyond the grasp of logic alone.

God created humanity in a similar "trinity" in his image, in a perfect balance of spirit, soul, and body (1 Thes 5:23). The spirit is our deepest and most essential being, beyond sensual form, emotions, or ideas. The soul is our self-awareness, the energy of who we are in God. Our mind is a tool to help us see our real self. Our body is the sensual and emotional house for mind and soul. The harmony of God works in us when these three separate, but intimately linked, aspects of our personhood are working in right order and priority.

The Book of Genesis teaches that humanity at the beginning had an awareness of perfect communion with God and with all creation. There was a total oneness in the diversity of all the various aspects of our own being, all species of animate and inanimate creation, and all individuals of human life. All was perfect concord and peace. All was beautiful music.

But somehow we got the idea that we could make better music on our own, without God. We reversed the priority of spirit, soul, body, and the world has seemed upside down ever since. Now we function with the senses and emotions of the body first, followed by the cognitive awareness of the mind. Unfortunately, the spirit of humanity was lulled to sleep, covered up, hidden. We, and all creation with us, lost awareness of our oneness with God.

I like to use the example of a light controlled by a rheostat to describe this. Before the fall, or the time that we tried to live separate from God and the things of the spirit, the light was turned all the way up. We could see things as they *are*. After the fall, it is as if the lights of creation had been turned all the way down with the rheostat, but not totally off. So we can see, but not as clearly as we were originally made to see. We can see truth, but only a small bit of it, "as if through a glass darkly," as Saint Paul also put it. The point of all religion is to help us rediscover this original gift and to restore us to our original state of completeness. Good religion brings us from the dim light into bright light. It is a tool for enlightenment. It helps bring us to authentic awakening.

To return to the musical analogy, all religions seek to get to the root of this problem of discord. They all recognize that something essential has been lost or covered up. They all point the way back, and forward, to the perfect harmony of divine music again. They all more or less agree that this can happen only through total death to the old self and the rebirth of a new person in that original harmony where the spirit is primary. They often use different language and metaphors to describe the process, but it is very much the same. In Christianity, we look to Jesus' promise to "make all things new."

Jesus came to reestablish fully that original music of God in complement to all that has come before or since, and in perfect completion. Rather than only pointing the way to reestablish the original music of God, or even just teaching the way, he actually *is* the way, the truth, and the life in his cross and resurrection. This is utterly unique among the religions. It is utterly beyond words, emotions, or senses to describe it, though it includes and fulfills them all.

I invite you to enter fully into this way of Jesus so that our lives may all reestablish this original music of God on the face of this earth. Through meditation and contemplative prayer let go of the discordant noise of your false self, no matter how attached you are to this false self-identity. Let your deeper and real self emerge through the ultimate self-emptying of Christ. Then you will hear the music of God everywhere and in everyone you meet.

Reality and Truth

Living from the hermit within not only opens our ears to God's music, but it also opens our hearts as well as our minds to what is real and true.

"But what is the truth?" This was Pilate's question to Jesus before his execution. Jesus says that we will know the truth, and the truth will set us free. He also promises us his Spirit to lead us unto all truth. Indeed, Jesus says that those who worship God must do so in Spirit and in truth. But what does he mean?

Most theologians say that his teaching does not apply only to an abstract objective truth about doctrines of faith and morality, though this is part of its meaning. It is really about ultimate Reality. We could easily use the word *reality* instead of *truth* in order to find its deeper meaning.

There is a certain objective truth to religion, to be sure. Most religions have dogmas of faith and moral absolutes. Christianity is no exception. Jesus lived, died, and was resurrected on the third day. These are objective truths that tell us who Jesus is. He also taught certain things about how we are to follow him, and he chose leaders from the general disciples to guide the community after he was gone.

These truths have been handed down through the church. Jesus chose the apostles, who installed successors to transmit the teaching as it had been received from Christ. A certain tradition was developed under the guidance of the successors to the apostles and Simon Peter. Eventually these primary teachings were written down and collected in the Bible. These are all objective truths about Jesus and how he wants us to live as his followers.

In Hinduism and Buddhism similar traditions developed. The Buddhists call it the Dharma Transmission. Dharma simply means the teaching, but it includes an intuitive understanding of ultimate Reality that can only be had through the experience of awakening. Yet it must be authentically transmitted through a teacher to ensure that serious mistakes are not made. Likewise, in Hinduism, submitting oneself to a teacher means actually receiving the spirit of the guru, called "standing on the shoulders of your teacher." A similar thing happens in Catholicism when we follow the successors to the apostles chosen by Jesus and receive the Spirit of Jesus as given to the church since the beginning.

But the fullness of the teaching is much bigger than a mere parroting of correct doctrine about Christian morality and faith. It is more than statements *about* the truth. The truth itself is mystical. It is beyond concepts, emotions, or form of any kind. It is a matter of spirit, and it must be spiritually intuited to be fully known. Most major religions include a mystical aspect that is beyond words. This is the truth that sets us free because it is not a phrase but a reality.

The mystical aspect of faith comes to us through paradox, an apparent contradiction that reveals a deeper truth. These paradoxes awaken the very spirit of humanity through a breakthrough experience. Examples of this would be finding eternal wealth through poverty, or hearing the word through silence, or finding ultimate communion through solitude, and so on. As Jesus taught, "The first shall be last, and the last shall be first." These truths all ring true on the deepest levels of our soul, though they seem like contradictions on the levels of thought, emotion, and senses.

These paradoxes break the shackles of the deeply ingrained habits and ideas of our false self. They take us back to the ultimate Reality for which we were originally created. They break us free of the bondage to the body and the confusion of our personal minds to the Reality of freedom with spirit-guided priorities for life.

Jesus is the ultimate paradox in his incarnation and paschal mystery. Especially in the latter, he no longer merely teaches these paradoxes as other great masters and religious founders have so often done. Here, he *is* the Paradox. He is the I AM who can finally awaken us to simply *be* in the ultimate Reality of Spirit.

When this happens, then our life falls into place. The senses and emotions and the concepts are not forgotten or discarded. On the contrary, now they begin to find their right place and can function in a healthy and productive way.

So what is *your* truth? Are you still trying to build a life from the outside, or have you discovered the key to happiness within? Are you climbing a ladder to nowhere, or are you listening to God where you are? Are you hearing the sirens of the world or the voice of the hermit within?

When you become still and silent and move beyond statements of truth to the Truth itself, you will come to know the Reality that is beyond all words, and it is this that will set you free.

The World Is Your Cloister

We are living in a time when many community structures are coming apart. Neighborhoods, families, and monasteries are dissolving. It remains to be seen what will fill the void as some of these things disappear. You might think that being a hermit, even an inner hermit, would free us from the obligations and duties of maintaining such things. But even the hermit in these times must, more than ever, help shore up the good values and traditions from such institutions. The hermit's heart is ever separated from all, and united with all. Wherever he or she stands, the world is the hermit's cloister. And the hermit's salvation comes in community.

When we hear the call to follow Jesus as his disciples, we do so as a personal response to Christ. But as soon as we follow him, we discover that other people also show up. They appear at work, at the ballpark, on the street, everywhere. The initial response to the call of Christ is personal and intimate, but the call to keep on going is unquestionably communal. It involves a community of disciples called the church or the gathering. It involves everyone, everywhere, in one way or another.

The reality of following Jesus is always communal. The first disciples formed a community around Jesus. They were together when he was arrested. They were together when he was resurrected. They were together when the Holy Spirit descended at Pentecost. In Acts 2:4 they stayed together as an intentional community, which evangelized Jerusalem and grew. The only time they were split up was when they lost their courage in the face of the cross or were forced to do so through persecution.

Throughout history the human being is a predominantly tribal creature. Most of the great cultures of this world are familial and tribal. In the rising tide of the Far East today, the greatest honor in work is to sacrifice one's personal desires for the sake of the family business. The Hispanic culture also has a family-first tradition.

Most ancient civilizations were built around the centrality of the temple. Religion is what held them together. Only modern Western civilization has adapted a more secular model.

Accordingly, most classical religion is communal in nature. While there is a realization of the need for the solitude of the mystic, there is a de facto awareness of the communal nature of following a master. The Hindu *sannyasin* first follows a guru in an ashram or community before venturing out alone, and even then the *sannyasins* help one another in the journey. The Buddhist monastic and lay disciples take refuge not only in the Buddha and his teaching, Dharma, but also in the *sangha* (community).

The early Christian monastic tradition is built on a similar pattern. The monks joined a community to follow the instruction of an abbot and/or elder monks who were Christian spiritual masters. Once they joined, they found themselves with many other younger monks who were often far from perfect. Yet it is right there in that imperfection that the presence of the more perfect teaching of the masters was tested. That is why the monks vowed to stay with a local community for life, and why even Christian hermits live in solitude with the support of a community of other hermits.

This stands in radical contrast to the modern culture of the West. In the West the individual stands in ideological preeminence over the community. We have embraced individualism. We have become the culture of me and self, never really sacrificing for the sake of all. This kills the possibility for stable social relationships. It has vast ramifications throughout a culture. To quote John Paul II, we have become a "culture of death."

The Franciscan John Duns Scotus (1266–1308) taught the venerable notion of individuation. Individuation rightly recognizes the unique and unrepeatable gift of each individual person. It creates a positive attitude of reverence for human life and its entire process from beginning to end, and a further love and respect for all life. However, this precious gift is always seen against the more primary backdrop of the communal dimension of all creation, humanity, and religion. Everything affects everything. Everyone is related to everyone. This is the wonder of interdependence. It is not something to debate. It is a simple fact of nature.

Individualism, however, is individuation gone bad. Individualism places the rights of the individual over anything else. It places the individual above natural community. This creates a society of illusionary selves. This manifests in hedonism, consumerism, economic inequality, and violence. Death is the result, whether through gangs in the streets, domestic violence in homes, avarice in offices, the killing of the unborn, the lost youth in our schools, or the elderly in the wards of nursing homes before their time. Individualism is the root of a lot of evil.

Sadly, we must admit that contemporary religion in America has not been able effectively to counter the tide of this self-centered culture of death. The seeker-friendly mega-churches, the ultra-conservative, evangelical, and charismatic churches, as well as the mainstream Christian churches, temples, and mosques, and even the newly popular (in the West) Eastern religions, have all come face to face with an individualism and said nary a word. Even the more individualistic and noninstitutional New Age and self-help gurus have not effectively turned the tide of the breakdown of our society, no matter how many books they write or TV and web appearances they do.

What is the answer? The answer comes from the hermit within.

It is to persevere with the classical forms of religion that take us past enslavement to our false self through meditation, contemplation, and active life in the world as brothers and sisters, one and all. The doctrines, liturgies, and lifestyles of these religions develop through time, and we come to realize the limitations of an expression in another culture or time, but the essential Truth, or Reality, is still found in them. This is especially true for Christianity, for those who follow Jesus. Only when the personal self is understood as an illusion can any of the problems of individualism be effectively solved. Until then, it is all just words and religious curiosity. So we must simply persevere in what is real and lasting with faith and determination.

A vocation usually depends on the little things of daily life. As we say here at Little Portion Hermitage: whether or not someone makes it usually depends on whether he or she can grow a green bean for God! It depends on how well the person can work with others in the mundane realities of the garden, the kitchen, or the office, just as much, if not more, than whether he or she understands the ideology of our life. As Jesus says, "Those who are faithful in little things will be given the great." Community is the place where this is tested and perfected through daily life with others.

Many of us are inspired when we read about hermits and monks. But when it comes to actually living the life, even as an associate, we fall back and move away. This can come from a misunderstanding of the life of a modern hermit or monk. We often have overly romantic notions of monastic life and can be shocked when we find out that the ordinary things of life must first be dealt with in monasteries and hermitages too. A monk or hermit still has to pay bills for even a moderate use of this world's goods. Therefore, the hermit or monastery must find a way to work for a living. Gone are the days when royalty paid the way of the monks, sisters, and hermits. Modern monks must pay their own way through work, with a smaller dependence on the rich for the basics of our physical life.

I write from the perspective of an integrated monasticism. Today there is a renewed interest in the whole monastic and contemplative tradition of Christianity, and of other faiths as well. Perhaps people are tired of the "show biz," motivational-speaker overtones of typical modern churches and their perpetuation of the Middle American status quo as contrasted to what we read in scripture and historical Christianity.

But what is a monk? The word *monk* comes from the Greek word *monos*, which means "one" and "alone." It was originally used to describe those who went into the deserts of Egypt to renounce themselves completely in order to follow Jesus more perfectly. This movement was so pervasive that it literally swept through Christendom in a matter of years and called hundreds of thousands of the members and leaders of society into its ranks. It was clearly the religious phenomenon of its day.

At first the word *monk* applied to those who lived in strict solitude, silence, and poverty as hermits in the deserts of Lower Egypt (meaning those downstream on the Nile). Thus, the word applied literally to those who were alone. But as more joined this way of life the desert got crowded. Loose communities formed. But they were not strictly organized communities yet. These monks were inspired by Matthew's Gospel (chapters 10 and 19). At most they were loosely organized into colonies following the example of Saint Anthony of the Desert (251–356) and Saint Macarius of Alexandria (d. 395). They lived in caves or huts, about a day's walk from a church and common center where they all met once a week for a meal on Saturday and celebration of the Eucharist on Sunday. After that, they returned to their cells or the place where "celestial" realities came to earth until the next week.

Another stream quickly developed in Upper Egypt (those upstream on the Nile) under the leadership of Saint Pachomius (292–348). He organized the monks into a strict common life for those who felt called but could not live the strict seclusion of the other pattern. These communities developed into virtual monastic cities in the desert and had a profound effect on the civilization in which they were situated. These monks were called cenobites after the Greek word *koinonia* or "fellowship." They used the Acts of the Apostles 2:4 as their scriptural inspiration: "All of them were filled with the Holy Spirit."

While most of us are not necessarily called to join a monastery, these two ancient patterns of monks still have much to teach us today.

First, they teach us to live for God and God alone. Jesus clearly taught that we must renounce everything in order to follow him, and Saint Evagrius, the fourth-century monastic aescetic writer, offers the paradox that we must "renounce all to gain everything." Our smallest place of prayer is large enough to contain the entire world.

So what about us? Do we first give up the things we must use in order to use them properly? Do we still try to possess the people we love, or do we first let them go in order to love them without possessiveness in God? Finally, do we let go of our very self in order to find ourselves in the self-emptying divine love of Jesus?

Second, the monks of old teach us to establish a good daily environment in our life for God. The monks made their whole life a good environment for meditation and prayer. Do we use the tools given us by God to help make our whole life a beautiful prayer? Do we at least regularly go to church to immerse ourselves in an environment of prayer through word, sacrament, and fellowship? Do we have a prayer place at home? Do we set aside daily time for meditation and prayer? Do we carry the thoughts God gives into our family, our work place, our recreation?

Lastly, the monks teach us to find real and lasting unity with one another through our divestiture of self in Christ. But it must be asked: Do we really live in oneness, or communion, with our brothers and sisters in Christ, and the whole human family? Do we live in community, or are we really "Lone Ranger" Christians? We may love because we are told to. This is better than nothing. But better yet is to love because we have been transformed within and recognize our true self in our brothers and sisters everywhere.

May we learn the lessons of the ancients of the faith and apply them to our life today in a way that makes our whole life a prayer and something beautiful for God. When the world becomes our cloister, it is a place where the beauty of God shines.

The early Franciscan friars of the thirteenth century also taught us that when the world is our cloister, it becomes holy to beg. Now what is that all about? Are we going too far here? What are our notions of beggars? Do we see them as Christ coming to us under a special form of poverty, or do we see them as a drain on respectable society? Are they a gift from God or a scandal?

I never saw real beggars until I went to Jerusalem and saw them at Damascus Gate. Since then I have seen terrible poverty from developing countries to American streets.

I have said that I write from a monastic, hermit tradition. But I write also from the Franciscan heritage. Saint Francis of Assisi lived some eight hundred years ago and sought to follow Jesus and the gospel literally. Because he had the humility to start with himself, God used him to reform the whole Western church. Today people of all faiths love him.

Francis was part of what we call the mendicant movement in church history. It took place primarily in the thirteenth century in the West. This spiritual movement included what came to be known as the Franciscans, Dominicans, Augustinians, and many, many more.

Mendicant simply means "open handed" and refers primarily to the new religious communities raised up by the Spirit who begged in the name of the Lord. They begged with open hands. They approached God and the entire world as beggars, with open hearts and open hands.

Up until that time the monks of Europe worked at their trade in their monastery. While renouncing personal property, they owned all things in common as a community following the example of Acts 2 and 4. These new mendicant monks, usually called friars or brothers, were trying to follow the literal example of Jesus Christ, who owned nothing and lived off of the good will of the faithful during his ministry.

Relevant to your desire to express your inner hermit, understand that Francis was both a hermit and a beggar. He was in his cloister in the streets or in a hermitage. His cell was wherever he was, and his hermitage was wherever his soul found rest. Francis founded twenty-five hermitages all over the Umbrian and Rieti valleys in Italy. They were founded in seclusion, but not so much seclusion that the friars could not easily walk into the villages and towns around them and preach the word, even without words.

It was here that many people encountered Francis the beggar. The friars, or brothers, would go into the world during the day and retire to their hermitages at night to engage in deep meditation and contemplation. They practiced begging when work in the hermitage or in ministry was not enough to provide for necessities, but also for humility and for solidarity and support of the poorest of the poor. A similar integration of solitude and ministry can be seen in Hinduism and Buddhism with their "homeless" monks and their *sannyasins* or "renouncers."

Francis never envisioned a community of freeloaders. The friars were to work at their trade or minister through word, sacrament, or corporeal works of mercy to the poor. In exchange for their labor they might receive food and clothing for one day and night, but they could not accept money. Only when there was no work to be found could they turn to the "table of the Lord" as beggars.

The notion of begging had special significance in the socioeconomic climate of the day. Europe was just discovering the use of money as a means of exchange. Up until then most of the world used the barter system, with only an ancillary use of money. In the time of Francis the world had gone crazy over the new use of money. Francis showed that the brothers could have peace and happiness even without the accumulation of the newest technology of greed. He renounced the use of money.

Religious begging is not unique to Jesus and the apostles or to Christianity. It can be found in most of the major religions of the world. Buddhist monks are actually called *bhiksu*, which means "homelessness." They are also called mendicants. The male Buddhist monks originally spent the monsoon season in a monastery and spent about nine months a year on the road in homeless begging while sharing the Dharma. The *sannyasins* of Hinduism did the same, only they did not usually teach, for they walked in silence. Later they were permitted to teach and preach. Jesus clearly fits into this tradition of the homeless renunciant, as did the first disciples and apostles. The monastic reforms and the pilgrims of the Christian East tried to imitate Christ in this lifestyle, and so they also fit into this category.

What does this mendicant tradition have to say to us?

It teaches us to open our hands to God.

I often begin my retreats at Little Portion Retreat and Training Center by asking people to open their hands to God. I do the same at my concerts. In order to open our hands we have to let go of anything that we are still clinging to. It is often the little things that we clutch covertly, thinking that no one will see. But God sees. Only when we let go of absolutely everything can God do whatever he wills in our life. Until then we are trapped by the devices of our own making. We cannot get free.

Only when we let ourselves become beggars with Christ, Saint Francis, and the holy traditions of the entire world will we discover the greatest treasure ever to be known. It is the treasure of spiritual freedom, awakening, and rebirth. It happens when we let go of the old self, let the false person die, and allow ourselves to be born again. This is why Jesus says that we must be born again and become like a child to enter the kingdom of heaven. For Christians, this happens once and for all in the cross and resurrection of Jesus Christ in a way beyond mere teachings and words.

You, too, can become a mendicant for the Lord. Open your heart and hands to God. Pray in silence and then enter the cloister of the world without expectations and let God provide you with your thoughts, words, and right actions. When you live from your inner hermit, God will fill you with a spiritual abundance beyond anything that you ever dreamed possible.

Obedience

To make the world our cloister and live from the hermit within, it helps greatly to understand and follow, in our own way, the virtues practiced by monks throughout time.

Consider, we are bombarded with information. It comes to us through TV, the radio, through the Internet. We can now get updated on just about anything every few minutes. But are we really learning anything? We are accumulating knowledge but are we growing in wisdom? Scripture says that in the last days we will run to and fro, that knowledge and evil will increase, but we will not come to knowledge of the truth (2 Tim 3:7). Coming to knowledge of the truth implies *listening,* not just hearing.

Obedience is a timeless monastic virtue, and its root is listening. Listening is a contemplative experience. We must be silent to listen. We must listen to learn wisdom. We must be a contemplative. We must be obedient.

Obedience is not just about following orders. Sure, there is a functional obedience involved in the success of any good business or organization. The church, monasteries, and ministries are no different. Without obedience no organization can survive. But the obedience of the inner hermit must go deeper. It is a matter of the heart. It is a matter of the spirit.

In the monastery we often get people from military backgrounds. Some of the saints, like Ignatius of Loyola (1491–1556) or the great monastic cenobitic founder Saint Pachomius (292–348) had military backgrounds. In some ways this is good preparation for religious obedience. In the military one must obey. It is not a choice. It is a duty. But it is no secret that military obedience often involves some grumbling while actually doing what one is told. This is not enough for spiritual obedience.

Saint Benedict says that we must obey with cheerful hearts. This is easy when we like what we have been asked to do. It is tough when we don't. Sure, we can explain our position to our leaders when we are having problems, but sometimes they still ask us to do something we would not choose on our own. This is rough on the ego. Benedict goes on to say that even if we obey outwardly, if we grumble and complain inwardly, it is as if we were not obedient at all. The virtue starts with obedience to legitimate spiritual and civil leaders and branches out to all seniors, all members of a community, and all people. Ultimately, it is an expression of our obedience to God, who establishes all legitimate authority on earth for our well-being and good. Still, this is a tall order!

What does this mean to those who yearn to listen to their inner hermit?

It has been my experience that monastic obedience helps us let go of our ego and pride better than almost any other tool. It is tough, but the goal is simple. What is it that makes us grumble when we are unhappy with a job we have been asked to do? What makes us angry when we do not get our own way or when someone treats us in a way we do not like? It is the displaced ego, our false sense of self. When the ego gets its toes stepped on, we complain. Erase the displaced ego, and we can relate to others positively, and our emotions and thoughts can be used in a wholesome way.

Notice I say the *displaced* ego, not just the ego. To have no ego at all would mean losing our self-awareness. That is not the goal. The problem is not the ego. The problem is how we have allowed the ego to function. The goal is to get the ego off the throne at the center of our life, inviting God to reside there, and letting the ego take its place at the foot of the throne, serving God.

This reminds me of the old Campus Crusade for Christ tract. In it was a picture of a throne with the ego seated on the throne and Christ at the foot of the throne. Jesus was not out of the picture. He was still there, but he was in the wrong place! Likewise with us. We are often religious, or even good Christians. But Jesus is not really on the throne of our life. He is still subservient to the ego. When we let Jesus sit on the throne of our life, then the ego finds its right place. It is not out of the picture either. But now it is in a place that is healthy and life-giving.

Then our ego is no longer in control. It works as a servant of God, who is all-knowing and good. When we let go of this control and autonomous centrality (which is an illusion anyway), we find our life coming into right order and peace with God, others, and ourselves, maybe for the first time. It does not destroy us. It saves us from ourselves so that we might be ourselves as God created us to be. '

Jesus is the greatest example of this. Paul in Philippians 2 says: "Who, though he was in the form of God, did not regard equality with God something to be grasped. Rather, he emptied himself." Jesus says that his followers must also "renounce their very selves." Saint Benedict says that the monastic life is designed to help us overcome our "self-will." Saint Paul uses the language of the "old self." Today, some call it the "false self." It all means letting go of the person we have allowed ourselves to become, the person who is not according to the image of God. It is a fake person interested only in a fake self. This self doesn't make us happy. It doesn't make others happy either.

For the inner hermit this letting go of the displaced ego often happens first and most profoundly in meditation. For one who associates with a religious community but lives in the secular world, a good spiritual director is often a great help. That spiritual director is like an abbot in a monastery—spiritual father and mother, elder, mentor, and friend. Spiritual directors are there to guide, not to manipulate or control. They help us to avoid mistakes and to take advantage of successes in the spiritual life. They share with us what they have lived and learned. A good spiritual director is a gift from God and points the way to God. God is the ultimate spiritual director dwelling within each inner hermit. The human spiritual director simply directs us to God.

As those brought into our lives by God, we are wise to listen to our spiritual directors and, unless they teach against our conscience formed by the gospel through the church, obey them. We cannot lightly disregard them when they direct us in paths we may find uncomfortable or difficult. It is often in these difficult paths that we learn the greatest lessons about letting go of the old self. Growth isn't always comfortable.

Next, this letting go is tested and tried in daily life. In our community most people who come to our beautiful and rugged monastic valley in the Ozarks agree with the ideals of the community or they would not even go to the trouble to get here. (Situated over two miles from the nearest paved road and almost an hour from the nearest big town, we are hard to find!) It is in the little things of life that one's "death to self" is tested.

At Little Portion Hermitage we have to be able to do a job a little different from the way we would do it if we were in complete control. We work with folks we might not choose to hang out with in the secular world. Little by little, person by person, and conflict by conflict, our misplaced ego can be put back into its original place. But this is in no way easy. It is tough stuff, and it requires courage to persevere.

There are still conflicts and difficulties in the inner hermit's life. The difference is that one will now be able to process such things without the tension, stress, and anger that come from the misplaced ego. We can work out differences with others when we listen to our spiritual guides, rather than trying to get our own way or "getting back" at others for hurting us.

The inner hermit listens most of all to God. This is confirmed by the input of a good spiritual director. Hearing the voice of God (to repeat something worth repeating) happens by practicing stillness. Stillness is practiced first in meditation and prayer, and then in the midst of the activities of daily life. Breathing in and out, each activity of life becomes an opportunity for meditation and prayer. Eventually, there is no conflict between contemplation and action.

The inner hermit also listens to others. Having found God in profound silence, we do not feel the need to speak often when with others. When others speak, we make an effort to listen prayerfully. It is only when we listen that others will feel free to share, and only when they share that one will know what they think and feel, and what we think and feel as well.

But there is an art to listening. First, we hear their words. Next, we realize that different people are at different places in their spiritual journey. Some personalities are dominating. Some are endearing. Some come off gruff. Some barely come off at all. Listening requires getting beyond all that. We have to find a person's spirit, sometimes even before the person has found it himself or herself. If we keep God in mind as we listen, we let go of our own ego, and go to our own child of God within, to our true self. Then we are able to hear the child of God and true self beyond the misplaced ego within all others. Usually I find a teddy bear within the egotist, and a lion within the mouse. It is this person we must hear and call forth through our listening and our speaking.

When we practice meditation, prayer, and listening obedience, we discover that none of us is really independent. We are dependent on God for our very life. "In him we live, and move, and have our being." We are also interdependent with all creation, all humanity, the entire church, and every member of our primary family or community. None of us is an island. Every single thing we do affects every single other creature on earth for all time. And it all affects us. This is a wonderful mystery that enriches the lives of those who know it. To listen prayerfully to everyone in intuitive meditation and contemplation is really the only way to live effectively on earth. To shut ourselves off in prideful opinions, judgments, and egotism is illusory, and can lead to downright delusion. It is a way to destruction. Once we realize this, obedience becomes a simple fact. It is no longer an option.

So the way of obedience is very important to the inner hermit. It regards those in authority and those not. Mostly it is about mastering the art of listening and letting go of the old self in order to hear the thoughts of God. When we follow Jesus we can let go of our fake self and discover who we really are in him. We can become people who listen as a way of life, and so learn to speak more effectively. We become obedient sons and daughters of God.

We become what we already are: God's precious children.

Poverty

We're too busy. We multitask. We don't know if we're coming or going or already gone.

Gospel poverty is a way to help manage, simplify, and eliminate some of that clutter. It is a way to do an interior house cleaning. The means are both external and internal, but the goal is the same: to remove the clutter from one's soul.

Probably the best word for gospel poverty nowadays is *simplicity*. We all need to use worldly goods as long as we live in this world. Even monks and hermits have to live somewhere, eat, and make a living. Even those who live on alms must rely on the worldly goods of others. As Gandhi once said whimsically, "It takes a lot of people spending a lot of money to keep me in my poverty!" Someone has to earn a living.

For the inner hermit this poverty is evidenced in the simple act of meditation. It is a great value of gospel poverty to reduce our needs beyond simple food, clothing, and shelter to be able to be happy in life. We don't need to be rich to sit and breathe. Yet nothing more is needed. From that simple act we begin to find all the great mysteries of God, creation, humanity, and self. It is a lifelong work, but it requires nothing more than a blessed space big enough to sit and breathe and meditate and experience rebirth.

The rebirth of the spirit allows us to experience at least some of God's original plan for humanity. While senses, emotions, and thoughts are bound by time and space, our spirit is able to share in the Spirit of God, which is infinite and eternal.

This truly spiritual experience is beyond description, but it makes our whole life complete. So we embrace poverty to find the greatest wealth that can be known.

The senses, emotions, and thoughts are energies. We know them through faculties that can be explained by concepts and words. The spirit is pure essence and can only be experienced as pure intuition; it is, therefore, beyond description. We use words (as I do here) because it is all we have in this life, but always with a clear understanding that our words fall way short of complete explanation. All they do is point the way.

It is on the level of spirit that humanity shares in the divine life most fully while still here on earth. Here we share in God's omniscience, not because we know everything but because we can intuit everything in a way beyond ideas and concepts. The same is true of all of God's attributes, such as omnipresence, omnipotence, peace, harmony, beauty, joy, and especially love. Rather than making us proud, this makes us humble listeners—and just nicer folks to be around. Gospel poverty makes us better human beings.

The German mystic Meister Eckhart (1260–1328) describes the various levels of poverty. He begins with traditional levels such as simplifying one's life. But he ends with a description of poverty that is most profound and greatly misunderstood. He says that in the final stage of pure contemplation we experience "God beyond God." As soon as we describe God, we fall short. God gives us some revelation of the divine Self, to be sure, but our minds can never grasp the full revelation. So even calling God "God" falls short of God. This can only be done by the spirit in pure contemplation and can only be grasped by the faculty of intuition. To realize this is a great poverty of spirit and brings us to great humility before this mystery.

Most of the great spiritual teachers of the world teach that contemplation is found through some expression of paradox. When such a truth is spoken, one has an "aha" moment. We find wealth by embracing poverty, the greatest action in stillness, the greatest communication in silence, and so on. Poverty is one of these great paradoxes.

Jesus teaches the way of poverty, and he lived it. He says clearly that we must renounce all of our possessions. But he goes further and says that we must even renounce our relationships and our very selves as well. Why? Probably because we have done these things so poorly in the past, and these unhealthy patterns have become so ingrained that only complete renunciation will allow us to break free. Jesus on the cross is the ultimate example of poverty. It was there that he gave up not only possessions and relationships but also his very life. He not only *taught* the way of the cross, the way of poverty, but he actually *became* that way.

Scripture speaks of three basic models of poverty. The first is the complete poverty of Matthew 10 and 19: renouncing all possessions, whether personal, family, or communal. This was the model of Jesus and is also the model of the great renunciants of the great religions of the world.

The second is Acts 2 and 4: renouncing personal possessions but allowing for the community to retain common ownership. Most monasteries and subsequent religious communities used this in Catholicism, as did communities like the Amish, Hutterites, and the Brudderhoff in the Anabaptist tradition, just to name a few.

The last is 2 Corinthians 8: allowing for the basic human right to private property but sharing it freely with those in need, so that a certain equality results between rich and poor. This is the minimalist pastoral model for most believers. Even this model is rarely achieved; it is challenging. Inner hermits will fulfill at least the last model and may be called to the first two at times in their lives, or maybe even for life.

These models have radical societal ramifications regarding the gap between rich and poor, and the threat to world peace that often results from this growing gap. First, when we are ready to buy something, we ask ourselves whether it is a want or a need. This simple question will keep us from most of the purchases we make and stop any materialistic patterns in our life.

But God wants to give us some of our wants as well. A God of love, God wants to give us gifts and wants us to give one another gifts as well from time to time. The problem arises when we become addicted to our wants and think that they are needs. Then the problem is not only consumerism but addiction, which is really at the heart of consumerism in the first place.

As Pope John Paul II wrote in the encyclical *On Social Concern*: "All of us experience firsthand the sad effects of this blind submission to pure consumerism: in the first place a crass materialism, and at the same time a radical dissatisfaction, because one quickly learns—unless one is shielded from the flood of publicity and the ceaseless and tempting offers of products—that the more one possesses the more one wants, while deeper aspirations remain unsatisfied and perhaps even stifled" (no. 28). Has there ever been a clearer description of the emptiness of consumerism? He went on to say that when the many figure out that they have the little, they will eventually rise up in revolt to get at least what they need. This revolt may be peaceful or bloody. So, if inner hermits really believe in peace for self and for others, they will simplify their external lives as well as their internal lives of meditation and prayer. Otherwise their prayer and their solitude are a sham.

The last point is demographic. Most classical treatises on civilization reveal a rich local culture that is both rural and urban. Most folks were rural and produced the most basic thing we need to live: food. Others lived in the cities and produced the specialized things needed to help produce the basics more easily and to make life more civilized. Each local region covered most of its own major needs. There was also a healthy trade among regions and nations in specialized goods that made life more enjoyable.

There has been a major shift in the population of the world from the farm to the city and suburbs since World War II. This has placed an entire population far removed from the production of the basics of food, clothing, and shelter in order to survive. This means that, since fewer people are working more acres to produce foods for millions, we have to go thousands of miles to dinner every night. Why? When most people live on farms, the farms are smaller. Smaller farms allow them to grow more diverse crops in a more natural way. Thus, most of our food needs are produced in a local region. But when the minority of the people produces the majority of the food, they have to specialize with just a few crops and use less natural agribusiness methods. This means that the food produced in a local region is less diverse. To get a variety, we have to buy produce from farms far away.

This has very real environmental ramifications. We have to produce crops with less natural methods, and then transport them long distances. This consumes huge amounts of energy. To do this we must also preserve the food for the long trip, and for a long shelf life. The result is an unnatural process that brings toxins into our land and eventually into our bodies, leading to an unhealthy planet and unhealthy people. Inner hermits try to be instruments of peace and healing.

We need to return to a healthy balance between rural and urban. To do this is not to renounce progress but to use progress in a way that is healthy and sustainable. We also need to redistribute the wealth of the few in a way that respects the freedom of all so that the needs of the many might be met. This represents a loving attitude toward all God's people and toward God's creation as well.

Associated with this is the concept of ownership. When the few own the land and businesses, then the many become mere employees and renters. Even those who think they own their homes and businesses become enslaved to the bank that really owns the property. This means that the owners grow rich while the employees remain dependent on them for the basics of life. It is not entirely an overstatement to say that this is a modern version of slavery. The answer is for all to own everything, and for everyone to be a steward of the gifts of creation that belong only to God. It was the way of tribal cultures for millennia. This is idealistic, to be sure, but it is not impossible if we all come to a new understanding of reality. It requires a whole new step in the evolution of humanity, but it can be done. Though not fully attainable in this life, it can be at least substantially accomplished. Inner hermits do their best to try to spread the way of heaven, even while here on earth.

All of this speaks to the dangers of the very heart of our modern way of life. A few are speaking out. A few are listening. Inner hermits need to be aware of such realities and do what they can to change them for the better.

So, inner hermits are to embrace gospel poverty and radically simplify their life. Once we really do these things, we embark on a journey of faith on which God never lets us down. Jesus asked the disciples if they were ever in need after he sent them out without money or walking staff or food or drink, and they answered that they were always taken care of. Likewise, inner hermits will always be taken care of by God if we embrace this poverty that leads us, and all people, to the true wealth of God for all creation and every living soul.

Likewise, embracing this poverty awakens us to the born-again experience of the wonders of the human soul in the Spirit of God. This gives us courage as we wait for the full revelation where we will participate in the new heaven and new earth in full beatific union with God, and full communion with creation, humanity, and ourselves in Christ Jesus.

Chastity

We live in a promiscuous culture. But as troubling as this may be, the culture is not the main issue related to chastity for the inner hermit. Chastity (a virtuous fidelity that may or may not include celibacy) has more to do with the call of the inner hermit.

Inner hermits strive to keep their thoughts pure and emotions unruffled so that their inner spirit might emerge in the grace of God's Spirit in pure contemplation. Their goal is union with God. This is a most precious gift. It is grace.

Chastity as celibates or as faithful married couples is a normal way of life. The single life is open to marriage but is celibate until marriage. Celibacy in some form is recognized by most mystical and contemplative traditions of the world. It is primary in the monastic and hermit traditions. The word *monk*, as we've said, means "one" and "alone." The word *hermit* comes from *eremite*, which means "desert" and implies the solitary nature of the call. Celibacy for the monk is also an important aspect of meditation. For instance, celibacy is simply assumed in most serious meditation ashrams in India, whether one is married or not. Not being controlled by our sexual drive is essential to provide the right environment for attention and awareness of the stirrings of deeper thoughts and emotions, which in turn gives way to the deeper awakening of the spirit beyond all images, ideas, and words.

Chastity or fidelity in marriage is essential, especially in a society where promiscuity and multiple marriages are the norm.

For the major religions of the world marriage is the ultimate completion on earth of the male and female within us all. Catholic teaching is prophetic and mystical in this regard. It teaches that appropriate sexual activity has three elements:

1. *A complete emptying of ourself for another.* This is profoundly mystical. It is radically countercultural, to say the least. We find our greatest fulfillment in emptying ourself for the sake of another.

2. *A complete emptying of ourself for another within the context of marriage.* When one is spiritually, emotionally, and intellectually naked before another, going from one mate to another in this life cheapens the real mystical aspect of sexual union between two people. The sacred intimacy of sexual union in marriage is a glimpse of the inexplicable spiritual intimacy available among all in God during and after this life.

3. *A complete emptying of one's self for another within the context of marriage with the possibility of procreation under ordinary circumstances.* Chastity calls us to respect the natural process of the mystery of life from conception to natural end. Some couples cannot have children. This does not mean that they cannot enjoy sexual union and pleasure in marriage.

Again, to be properly understood, chastity is based on a mystical view of life, not on mere legal principle. Other traditions also see marriage as a mystical fulfillment of the male-female reality of the created universe. It is not to be toyed with by the immature or curious in sexual yoga, for doing so can end in sexual immorality and spiritual desecration.

Saint Paul recommends celibacy in marriage for a period of time, but only for as long as each partner wants to continue.

Conjugal chastity can be resumed afterward, but some have chosen continence for the rest of their lives.

Both marriage and the single life have a mystical meaning and are enriched by chastity. Chastity is a necessary beginning to greater steps of meditation and contemplation for the inner hermit.

There are also other expressions of chastity. Aiming for purity in whatever we ingest into the body is a wholesome practice, if not taken to extremes. Many are returning to organic and natural foods and breaking the patterns of addiction to food, drink, and substances. Fasting is a great way to purify the body. The church has traditionally fasted on Wednesdays and Fridays; there are other liturgical fasts throughout the year. These fasts can be total or partial. Monastic fasting involves eating less daily, limiting meat and cooked dishes, but not going completely without food.

The practice of chastity of thought in meditation is also important. By stilling the body through asceticism, posture, and breath, the body and mind calm down and settle. The image of the stilled pond is helpful here. Then we can see thoughts and emotions more easily as they enter. This kind of mindfulness brings mental purity or chastity.

A chaste mind can discern if these thoughts are wholesome or unwholesome, valid or invalid, loving or selfish. In a cluttered mind we often cannot tell if thoughts are helpful or harmful until they have already taken root, or until we have acted upon them with word or deed. A chaste mind is able to discern them much sooner and can keep the invalid ones from bringing harm into our lives, or into the lives of others around us.

St. Augustine calls this "nipping it in the bud." This is a good gardening analogy that rings true for any who have grown a tomato in the backyard or on a windowsill. To nip it in the bud means that we can reach down with our thumb and index finger and simply snap off the new shoot. It is easy and causes no serious damage to the plant. But when we wait too long, we must use shears, and it hurts the plant. This means that thoughts are easier to remove when they are new and just forming in our mind. Once they take root and spread they are much more difficult to remove.

The Christian does this out of love for Jesus. He is the bridegroom of our soul. When we allow darkness to enter our body and soul, we do damage to our love relationship with our eternal spouse, Jesus. We remain faithful and pure, not just for the sake of meditation and contemplation, but mostly out of love, just as we do for an earthly spouse. We would never think of being unfaithful to a spouse we love properly. When we are, it means that we do not properly understand deeper love, and we must work to heal the relationship. If we understand God's love for us in Jesus Christ, then we cannot help but respond with similar love. We cannot help but be chaste in body, soul, and spirit.

So the internal chastity of the inner hermit is not just about externals, though it includes them. It is about purity of emotion and thought so that we can open up with a rebirth, an awakening of spirit in the Spirit of God. This is a gift. We can do the work that God asks us to do to prepare, but real contemplation is given as a love gift by the grace of God. Once received, the inner hermit is sometimes filled with holy tears that become a well of salvation and a river of deep peace.

The Gift of Tears

⤴

Many have asked me what is the greatest fruit of religious reclusion—living in prayer and meditation apart from others for a period of time. I can answer without hesitation that it is the gift of tears.

Those who embrace this more solitary life find this gift rather common. I think it is because by moving into great solitude beyond the world of human judgment and approval or disapproval, we are freer to respond in complete honesty to the things of God. The things of God—goodness, truth, beauty, love—bring a humble soul to tears of sorrow for shortcomings, and, most of all, tears of joy for the unconditional love of God.

The simple thought of Jesus dying for us out of such great love sometimes moves even the hardest heart to tears. If the thought of another human being dying to save our life without expecting anything in return moves us to tears (and it usually does—ask any war vet), so much more does the thought of the most innocent and pure human in all history dying to save us from death.

The trouble is that we rarely let down our defenses enough to set the soil for such an experience. The way of reclusion is an inspiration for those of us following the way of the inner hermit. While we may not all have the time and place for such uninterrupted honesty, we do at least get snatches of it in times and places of solitude and silence. These sacred times and places can easily become times and places of holy tears.

I am reminded of Paul Simon's song "The Cool, Cool River." One of the lines says, "Sometimes even music cannot substitute for tears." There are both healing tears and unhelpful tears. Unhelpful tears keep us stuck in the past. Good tears wash us clean so we can be grateful for the present and assuredly face the future. But there are times, in the midst of tears, when we cannot easily tell the difference. We just have to let it work for a while. Then the healing will come.

For me, tears are inseparably linked to meditation and contemplation. Through meditation we are sometimes able to silence the ceaseless chatter of our thoughts. When this happens, we are more capable of seeing what's real. Bodily senses stop jerking all over the place and become stable houses for the soul and spirit. Emotions are silenced. God whispers to us, with or without words. At this point I begin to weep.

I am utterly grateful for being allowed to live this way of life in general, and in religious reclusion in particular. Often when praying the Divine Office, or doing sacred reading *(lectio divina)*, I weep because I am able to take these at my own speed. I am not sure that this would be healthy if I had not first spent twenty years praying the Divine Office and attending mass or a communion service almost daily. Through the communal celebrations one finds the discipline to do them whether we feel like it or not. That choice was made when we came here to live. But once we have "gotten it," after twenty or so years, then we can retire into a deeper hermitage of reclusion. I now can slow liturgy down a bit. When this happens, the tears come.

Sometimes I am reduced to tears when reading a wonderful book. The book is almost always spiritual and monastic in content. It may be the holy scriptures. At a certain point I can simply let the book rest in my lap, and meditation moves toward contemplation, which is beyond images, forms, names, or agendas. At that point tears might come as well. I often find that just resting a time-tested book on my lap after reading a few lines is sufficient. When I was younger, I was a voracious reader, and I remembered almost everything I read. Now that I am older, I find quality far superior to quantity. Reading becomes a preparation for contemplation.

I also find myself going back to the basics. One stage of prayer that is always coming back to me is tears for forgiveness and salvation. I have really done some stupid things in my life, both in my rock-and-roll days and in my Christian days. But it is in founding this integrated monastic community that I have experienced the greatest hurts of my life, and hurt others as well.

This life of reclusion has allowed me to weep for those hurts and mistakes. I weep for myself and for those I have hurt. There is no room for excuses in a recluse's hermitage. All that is present is God and me. It is a place for honesty before God, and God's honesty to me. At this point I weep for my sins and am left stuttering and stammering that God actually forgives me. There are no more words. Only tears will do.

I have heard that there is a brother on Mount Athos who weeps, smiles, and says nothing but, "What do you think, brother? Are we being saved today?" This brother is considered one of the most advanced on his holy mountain.

Most of us are not called to live on Mount Athos or with the Camaldolese or with the Franciscans. Most of us are called to find an inner hermit right where we live, in our own house, our own family, our own parish, and in our current job. Most of us cry tears from time to time, but they are not the gift of tears. They come from unforgiven hurts deep inside that we often carry for many years or even a lifetime.

Unforgiving tears—when we don't forgive or experience forgiveness—hurt us. They become anger, and when anger is not healed it comes out as bitterness. We think that we are hiding our pain and hurt from others. But in fact everyone can see or intuit the hurt, the anger, and bitterness in our countenance, our forced smile, our superficial speech and jokes.

Yet, if we set aside a daily time and place for Christian meditation, and seek out some pastoral care and healthy spiritual direction, these unwholesome tears can be changed from something that blinds us to something that cleanses and heals us and opens our heart as well as our eyes.

This is the gift from God witnessed to by the lives of the great hermit saints. And it can be yours as well.

Transformation of the World

> In the world you have tribulation, but take courage; I have overcome the world.
>
> —JOHN 16:33

> Therefore, if anyone is in Christ, he is a new creation; the old has gone, the new has come!
>
> —2 CORINTHIANS 5:17

The world is a terrifying place. It's enough to make you cry tears of sorrow. It is also "charged with the grandeur of God," as the poet Gerard Manley Hopkins wrote. The secret is to transcend the terror by seeing the grandeur. As we see, so shall we be. That vision within us can light up the world and make all things new.

The Cistercian Thomas Merton used to travel from the monastery into the city of Louisville when he was a young monk. At first everything of the world seemed repulsive. But in prayer he learned to see. Later, when he went to town, he was astounded at how beautiful everything was. He stood on a corner one day, and it was as though the entire city glimmered with the grace of God. "How do you tell people," he asked himself, "that they are walking around shining like the sun!"

In the movie *Field of Dreams* a tourist asks the hero Ray Kinsella (Kevin Costner), "Is this heaven?"

"No," he says. "It's Iowa."

Now neither Louisville nor Iowa are literally heaven, but when we have eyes to see, all things become new and we behold a new heaven and a new earth right in front of our eyes.

We are now "in the world, but no longer of the world." The world has become our cloister.

Our actual experience of the presence of God is beyond the world. God gives us creation to lead us to the Divine, but once we actually experience the pure presence of God, that presence complements, completes, and surpasses all concepts, images, and ideas we have of God.

The world religions have many names for God, but they are not magical incantations. They only point to God's presence. Awareness of that presence is what is important. We revere the teachings of the church about God, creation, and humanity. They form the bulwark of orthodoxy, or right praise, and aid us in both right living and right spirituality. But they are not the actual experience of God. They are the indicators, the signposts, and the means of that spirituality. As my friend Mike Leach says: "Doctrines *about* the truth are not the truth. Like the Zen Master said, the finger pointing toward the moon is not the moon. Doctrines are fingers pointing in the right direction. And that is why we need them!"

There is no box big enough for God. We have to call this all-powerful, all-knowing, all-present Being *something,* so it is valid for Christians to call him God, for Jews to praise Yahweh, and for Muslims to pray to Allah. But we must realize that God cannot be limited to names, forms, ideas, and statements. These are given by God to lead us to God. But they are not God. They are only tools.

The presence of God is a pure experience. It is beyond images, ideas, or forms. The presence of God is a pure presence of Spirit within us. In this sense the presence of God is God beyond God. It is the knowing of what is Real, here and now.

That is what Thomas Merton realized on that street corner in Kentucky. That realization sprang from the soil of his perseverance in prayer and silence.

And that realization, if only for a moment, can come to us.

Holy Forgetfulness

Forgetting things is a normal part of the aging process. At least that's what my doctor tells me. So with every year I forget a little more. I can go to the kitchen and forget why I went there. I once forgot a guitar when going to a concert. I sometimes lose my place in concerts with songs I have sung for decades. My father used to tell me, "I have forgotten more than you know." I now know exactly what he meant!

But there is also a rich Christian tradition about forgetting. The author of *The Cloud of Unknowing* speaks of "the cloud of forgetting." First, we need to see forgetting as a way to clear the clutter of our mind so we might better focus on the thoughts that come from God. This is mostly a tradition of renouncing the things of the world so we might hold on to Christ and Christ alone. Here we employ the tools of word, sacrament, and asceticism. From the monastic stream we realize this through a moderate use of fasting, vigils, manual labor, spiritual reading, and meditation on God and the things of God.

We also realize the paradoxical tradition of finding knowledge in unknowing, divine light in divine darkness, wealth in poverty, speech in silence, companionship in celibacy, freedom in obedience, and so on. The Rule of Romuald for hermits teaches us that holy things remembered so deeply in the soul can be retained through forgetting. "Put the whole world behind you and forget it."

What are we to retain and what are we to forget, and how do we do it? First, we are to die to the things of our life that are not like Jesus. Here we might read and then meditate on Jesus and his life on earth, or his place in the blessed Trinity, and how to let go of our obsessive thoughts through a complete following Jesus in the here and now. We do this by embracing sacred reading and meditating on our reading in a way that leads to silence so that God can speak to us, or rather, that we can begin to hear God, for God is speaking to us always in the Word that is beyond but includes all words.

The goal is to let God achieve in us the only goal that will bring us peace: "Not my will, but thine be done." The goal is to let God see for us, so that, like Thomas Merton, we can see God's children "walking around and shining like the sun."

Only when the ego is forgotten can we say: "I can do all things through Christ who strengthens me" (Phil 4:13). And then it is not us, but Christ, who makes all the difference.

Practice in the Presence of God

> *Above all realize that you are in God's presence. Hold your heart there in wonder as if before your Sovereign.*
>
> —SAINT ROMUALD

In solitude and prayer, we begin to realize what we were taught as children: God is everywhere. Scripture tells us that he is present even in hell (Ps 139:8). What matters is our relationship in God's presence.

The Rule of Saint Benedict says so well: "We believe that God is present everywhere and that the eyes of the Lord behold the good and the bad in every place." So God is especially present when the monks pray together. Again, it is a matter of relationship.

God is everywhere. The purpose of meditation and prayer is to become aware of that presence and live in relationship with God. It is not so much that God "fills us," even though scripture uses that language to describe it from our perspective. God is already here. We simply enter into a relationship by being in the Presence of the One who Is.

How do we do this? Are there special sacred places in our life that help us to this awareness and relationship?

First, let us recall those special places and times that nurture our prayer life. In Little Portion Hermitage the church is a central place for many reasons. First, it is where the Blessed Sacrament and scriptures are reserved. These are God's special gifts to us. Second, it is the place where day after day, year after year, we people come to pour out our hearts to God in faith, hope, and love. This makes a place holy. We can absorb some of that holiness if we enter such places in reverence and open-ness. We also pass on our own experience of faith, hope, and love as we pray and worship there.

The Rule of Saint Benedict also speaks of holy times. Benedict set aside certain times to pray every day. These times find their tradition in early Christianity and Judaism before it, recommending seven times a day for prayer. Even the earliest Christians prayed the Our Father three times a day, morning, noon, and night. Muslims encourage five formal times of prayer a day. Most of the major religions encourage special times throughout the day for more formal prayer. Beyond holy days like Easter, Christmas, special feast days, and the weekly Sun-day worship, the church recommends that morning and evening prayers form the "hinges" of the daily Divine Office.

For those in the world living from their inner hermit this reinforces the idea that, beyond local church services, morn-ing and evening prayer and meditation time is very important. At the monastery we would add this in addition to our praying of the monastic Divine Office. For those at home something similar is always the ideal, but many simply cannot find this amount of time while getting home from work, school, and getting the family fed and off to any special extracurricular activities at church, school, or sports. For most, a morning and evening time of scripture reading and devotion, followed by quiet meditation and even contemplation, is the norm. If followed faithfully, this will bring forth great spiritual fruit after a time.

But it is even more important to practice living in the pres-ence of God. In the Christian tradition this has been popular-ized in the book *Practicing the Presence of God* by Brother Lawrence, a simple cook who reached great spiritual heights by simply remembering that God is always present. It is very similar to the classic *Sacrament of the Present Moment* by Jean-Pierre de Caussade, or, more recently, *The Power of Now* by Eckhart Tolle. All these books teach us to be awake in God's presence around us at all times. It is what Jesus meant when he taught us to "watch and pray always" (Lk 21:36).

This is also similar to what the Buddhists call mindfulness. Specifically, they talk about "stopping and realizing" at every moment and with every movement. In other words, they are aware that they are eating, talking, thinking, feeling, doing. From prayerful awareness comes gratitude.

Followers of Jesus call this awareness watchfulness. This means being aware of Reality in every moment. First, we are aware of the presence of God and our relationship with him. Next, we are aware of every movement in our body, soul, and spirit, senses, emotions, and thoughts.

This takes a lot of attention at first. It requires discipline and patience. We do this intentionally at first and at various specific times for practice throughout our life. But once we get the hang of it, we begin to do it as second nature at all times and in every place. Then, instead of cramping our style, it becomes a practice of liberation and self-expression. It makes every moment a moment to love God and all creation.

Practicing the presence of God makes every moment a prayer and an ongoing meditation. We move through the energies of body to the essence of spirit. Then, from the rebirth of the spirit within us we move back out through thoughts, emotions, and senses enlivened in the Spirit of God. Ultimately, with the help of God's Spirit, all life becomes a miracle as we are lifted up on the wings of the constant presence of God.

It is not so much that we find God. God finds us. God does not fill us because we let God do so. God is already there. We simply awaken to that realization. As the classic *The Cloud of Unknowing* says, God is not "up" or "down," "in" or "out."

God cannot "fill" us. We are already in God. These are only words that help express our relationship with God, who is already present everywhere as Love. We simply enter in to what has been the Reality all along.

Holy Emptiness

Empty yourself completely.

—Saint Romuald

Awareness of God within us and around us leads to emptiness. God's grace fills us when we are empty of ego. We become alive in Christ only when we are dead to our false self.
Scripture encourages this emptiness. As Saint Paul writes to
the Philippians of the work of Jesus: "Though he was in the
form of God, he did not regard equality with God something
to be grasped. Rather, he emptied himself, taking the form of
a slave, coming in human likeness; and found human in appearance." By becoming less, Jesus became All.

Holy emptiness is not to be confused with psychological
emptiness. Psalm 90 in the Office of Readings says, "Our
span is seventy years, or eighty for those who are strong. And
most of these are emptiness and pain." But it continues: "Make
us know the shortness of our life that we may gain wisdom of
heart." So the emptiness that is suffering can be a springboard to the emptiness that sets us free.

To write about meditation we have to allow ourselves to
become an empty page. Icon painters point out that white is
the absence of color. Black is all colors at once. White represents the letting go of everything so that God can use whatever "color" God wants. I try to do the same thing as a writer.
I sit in meditation for a while before I start to write. I meditate
until the white page becomes my spiritual center again. This

seems something akin to iconography, at least as I understand it.

An iconographer sometimes starts with a black or very dark surface. Some have said that this represents the sin of a fallen world. How? It is all the colors of the world used at once, insensitively and incorrectly. The result is a lifeless darkness. Then the iconographer brings it to life with the brilliant colors that represent the light of Christ that erases the sin of the beholder. Christ turns this darkness into beauty. This is a profound happening.

I'm reminded of this when I make music. Often I start with a beautifully simple song. But sometimes I get so many ideas that by recording them all the song ends up a jumbled mess of noise. What started out simple ends up complicated; what was beautiful is now downright ugly. In our final mixes we always take almost as much out as we leave in. To make good music one must know what to include and what to leave out. What is left out may be a great idea in itself. But that does not mean it is a great idea for a song. Good meditative songs are just as much about what you do not include as about what you actually hear in the final version.

This teaches me about an aspect of sin. Sin is trying to have everything all at once without allowing the deeper spiritual emptiness of light itself. It wants everything to the point of leaving no breathing space at all. We are afraid to risk emptiness. We are afraid to let go of anything we have so avariciously acquired, but we can never truly live with such an exclusively external attitude either. We need to get to the divine power of light. Sin cannot exist in the light.

Many of us suffocate from the seeming endlessness of the externals of the phenomenal world. We cannot empty ourselves of this burdensome blackness in the self-emptying of Christ unless we open ourselves to this gift. The emptiness of light is too spiritual for us when we only want to live in the phenomenal world. So we stay in the life-sucking blackness of what we mistakenly call "having everything."

The abundance of Jesus is much different. In contrast to the above analogy, a more modern scientific tradition says that pure white light includes all the colors when seen through a prism. It is beautiful and life-giving. It begins in the blessed poverty of letting go of all things, relationships, and even the self we think we are. Only then can we find our true self in Christ. Only then can we find the real spiritual wealth that the poverty of Jesus brings.

In order for the spiritual and phenomenal worlds to come together in harmony there must be both color and empty space in every form. In order for words to give life they must be imbued with silence. In order for form to be constructive it must serve space, for it is in space where life unfolds. It is in the room where life is lived, not in the walls. But we need the walls and the space to clarify various spaces for the wonderful varieties of abundant life. Where there is space and color, then a full spectrum of beautiful colors can inspire us spiritually, emotionally, intellectually, and sensually.

If we can but imitate the self-emptying of Jesus, we let go of this seeming reality of the phenomenal world. As we let go of this blackness, which seems to be all life at once but is only a road to death, we suddenly find our spirit and soul set free again. We can walk without the terrible burden and weight of the delusion of "having it all in the world."

Empty yourself completely. And say with all the saints, "It is no longer I who live but Christ who lives in me!" (Gal 2:19).

Contentment

Be content with God's gift.

—SAINT ROMUALD

Be content. This is difficult for those of us still struggling to let go of the ego, but it is a final steppingstone to spiritual progress. It doesn't happen all at once. It is a daily process. As Jesus says in so many different ways, we must carry our cross daily and lose our ego in order to find ourselves in him. This does not mean hating our real God-given self. It means seeking with all that we are the grace of God that restores this original self to awareness. This is the basis of our experience of the cross and resurrection of Jesus. We die in order to be reborn. The false self dies. The new self, created by God, is reborn in Christ.

This death to the old self can be initially painful. The displaced ego dies hard. It kicks and screams to be left as it is. It is like a drug we have become addicted to. We are comfortable with old patterns of behavior even when they are killing us. Ultimately, we are not really happy with the old self, and those who have to live around us aren't either. We must take the plunge and let it go. Soon enough, if only for a moment at first, the pain of this conflict begins to ease. And we know that if it is possible once, it is possible always.

This is where real contentment is found. If our goal is: "It is no longer I who live but Christ who lives in me!" (Gal 2:19), then we rest in the contentment that "I can do all things through

Christ who strengthens me" (Phil 4:13). When we decide to let go of the old self, then the struggle to hang on to our old ways (even religious ones) starts to diminish and substantially disappear. When all we seek is the freedom of the cross, then contentment finds us.

One of our sisters told of a time she was complaining about the crosses of her life to her confessor. He said: "Why are you complaining when you say you embraced this way of life to find and embrace the cross! Why are you complaining because you got what you asked for?" When we carry the cross of our ego in order to die to it and rise again, we know the contentment of Christ.

Where do we find these crosses? First, when we confront our patterns of egoism through various ascetical disciplines, we find an opportunity for joy and peace. But the greatest contentment is when there is no bruised ego to complain at all. Since the ego is found in its proper place as a servant of God, it is content no matter what happens to it. This does not mean becoming a zombie or robot. But it does mean discerning the love, joy, and peace in every situation of life. As Saint Francis said, "Since we possess nothing, we are everywhere at home." We are always content. We are, says Saint Romuald, "like a little chick tasting and eating nothing but what its mother brings."

I live most of my life in a hermitage within Little Portion Hermitage. We are a community dedicated to radical gospel living and prayer. The semi-eremitical way of life is our primary pattern. But when I travel in my music and teaching ministry, I venture out into the secular world. I come face to face with all the sensual and ego temptations of the world. This gives me great love and sympathy for those whose life vocation bids them to bring the gospel into this world, especially in the rampant consumerism and egoism of the modern West. Life can so easily become an endless array of technological toys and sensual comforts. We men—*and* women—fall too easily into the "boys and their toys" syndrome.

I once asked a prominent newscaster in a nearby city what people did in his town? He said, "They own restaurants." When I asked what they did for recreation, he said, "They go to other people's restaurants, and go out to see movies." Life becomes lived secondhand. And yet it is enticing. Every local area has restaurants from the major cultures of the world. Things that were once considered delicacies are now considered common. Today's gadgets are yesterday's science fiction. It seems irresistible.

Good food and technology are not bad, but a culture of obese people addicted to food and passive entertainment is. Technology is good, but technological "junkie-hood" is not. We cannot find fulfillment there. Even "sex, drugs, and rock 'n' roll" are okay in the right context, but illicit sex and substance abuse are killers. I still like a bit of old time rock 'n' roll, but too much of it brings out a coarseness in my spirit that is an obstacle to deeper spiritual growth.

The deeper spiritual life calls us to external and interior silence and solitude that open us to the real abundant life of God. They call us to deny the false nourishment of egotistic junk food and to seek out real spiritual food. This means sometimes cutting ourselves off from the sugar-coated food of the secular world in order to find the real meat of the gospel. The sugar might seem to taste better, but it will kill us when eaten exclusively or to excess.

For me, this has meant living a simple way of life that provides the environment for eremitical prayer and communal charity. At first, and at various times of temptation, I have longed for the pleasures and luxuries of the secular world just like everyone else. But the longer I have lived this life, the more content I have become in it, and the less I have longed to leave it . . . more content than I ever was riding the waves of

secular success. I have come to treasure the solitude and silence, the poverty, chastity, and obedience, and my brothers
and sisters in community who share this way of life with me.
After the initial years of struggle, I have become content.

Even eating is a symbol of how a change in viewpoint can
lead to perseverance in better habits, which leads to mindfulness, which in turn leads to contentment. I was raised in trav-
eling folk groups and rock bands, so I learned to eat as a
young adult in truck stops all across America. We usually had
thirty-minute stops in which to order and eat, so I learned to
eat really, really fast! In monastic living I have found that when
I take the time to slow down I am able to really enjoy the taste
of the meal better, and I eat less. Eating slowly allows me to be
mindful of and thankful for the blessing of each mouthful, not
to mention each meal, and everyone and everything that went
into bringing it to the table. I am also more mindful of those
who do not have enough to eat on a given day.

When I eat like this, I discover that I am not that hungry
most of the time. After all, I get three square meals almost
every day. Even on fast days I find I have plenty. So I am not
that hungry. Simply becoming aware of this has completely
changed my eating habits.

This is a state of mind. If we think of ourselves as hungry,
we will be hungry. If we eat mindlessly, we will become mindless and slowly come to think of ourselves negatively. If we
think of ourselves as a slob, we become a slob. If we think of
ourselves as fat, sick, and run down, we will be overweight,
unhealthy, and tired. But if we think of ourselves as satisfied,
we will not be hungry. Then we will not overeat. Then we will
have more energy and be content.

The same is true for being content with what God gives. If
we live unmindfully we fill up our lives with all kinds of intellectual, emotional, and sensual stuff that we do not really need.
The sad thing is that we think that we have to have it. We

cram our lives with junk food, get fat, and remain essentially unsatisfied. This is classical addiction. And it happens to the ego in the same way.

If we live mindfully in the sacrament of the present moment, we still have spiritual, intellectual, emotional, and sensual needs. But because we have gone through an "ego detox" program, we can discern what our real needs are. God gladly meets those needs. And we can be truly content with what God provides. It may be radically different from what we are used to with the habits of our old self. But instead of being based on illusion and desire, it will be based on reality and need, and it will give us life and set us free.

Living with a spirit of contentment is truly liberating. Instead of thinking of ourselves as miserable, our self-image changes to one of contentment and peace. And the more our self-image changes, the more we enter into it. It is an upwardly moving spiral staircase in godly living. We can be in a situation that encourages overindulgence in spirit, intellect, passions, or senses, but we will remain content and peacefully free not to indulge. This is liberation. This is being set free. This is being content.

In eremitical reclusion I am learning that so much of what I think I want or should do in a given day is just a waste of time. Even in the hermitage we can fall into the trap of "doing for God." God does not need our works. God only wants us. Then the works will follow. But so much of even our religious life is not really born of God's will for us. All that is needed is to sit at the feet of the Lord in adoration and love. As Saint Teresa of Avila said, "I look at him, and he looks at me." That is all. In perfect love no more is required. As Jesus said, "Mary has chosen the better portion, and it will not be denied her" (Lk 10:42).

When we can be content with living in the presence of God, then we can be content wherever we are. We can be content in trial or security, poverty or wealth, war or peace, solitude or community, silence or speech, in recognition or in being over-looked and ignored. The list goes on and on. And the list of reasons for discontent is also endless as long as our ego and our wants are in control. When we let go and let God, when we die with Christ by carrying his cross daily, then we are born again and have contentment beyond measure.

So, whatever the pace of our progress, we can be content with where we are. This does not mean growing complacent, or giving ourselves permission to stop growing and stand still. It just means being patient with our own humanity, and going forward in God's time.

The anonymous writer of the Carthusian classic *They Speak by Silences* says, "We must be content with everything—even with being discontented! We must get right out of ourselves, forget ourselves, so renounce ourselves that whether we are contented or discontented no longer matters, but only the good pleasure of 'Him Who Is.'"

In the early days of our community we spoke of finding "stability in instability." This is similar. We must not only find the wealth of poverty, but also find poverty in wealth; not only the Word in silence, but also the silence in words; not only communion in solitude, but solitude in communion; not only freedom in obedience, but obedience in freedom.

I cannot tell you the hours I have spent trying to bring peace to young aspirants who are frustrated with themselves to the point of constant agitation. This muddies their spiritual vision. Soon, since they are unhappy with themselves, they begin to judge all those around them. In the end they must either learn to be patient and find contentment with themselves and oth-ers or leave the community. When they do not learn this les-son, it is always very sad, for this problem will follow them wherever they go until they do learn it.

This is especially important for the inner hermit who lives in the world. God is perfect, but the fallen world is imperfect.

Expecting perfect contentment immediately or too soon will leave one very discontent because perfect contentment simply does not exist in this world. The same is true for solitude, silence, and poverty. We must always strive to do better, but we must not lose our contentment when we do not do as well as we had hoped. What is important is to try our best with the grace of God. Then, as always, we must simply love ourselves and others in the presence of God.

Persevere

Perseverance, sticking to it, is a real challenge for anyone, and great virtue for everyone. American lives are revolving doors of activity. Some people go from relationship to relationship, job to job, and church to church. We thrive on novelty. It is healthy to have the freedom to grow, but not when all this flittering ruins the basic fabrics of civilized life. We need to persevere in values and practices that increase our quality of living and give room for our inner hermit to grow.

Benedictines and other monastic traditions have always stressed perseverance in praying the psalms. The psalms are important because they bring out the rich diversity of human responses to God. But the call to stay the course of spiritual practice is not limited to praying the psalms or meditation or any one thing. It applies to celebrating the sacraments, the signs of God's mystery in our lives. It applies to devotions such as the Rosary that are meaningful and helpful to us. It applies to any spiritual disciplines or ascetical practices that help us to curb our unruly tendencies to get lost in mindless activity.

Most spiritual practices will eventually lose their freshness and become a source of boredom and tedium. But it is precisely there that our faith and determination are tried, and it is only through grace-filled faith and perseverance that we are able to reach the hidden treasures of these practices. It takes time—day after day and year after year—before these treasures come to light. We must stick to it.

I am reminded of what the Zen Buddhist tradition teaches: we need great faith to believe, great doubt to ask the right questions, and great determination to persevere. Its proponents would add that in order to get at the marrow of spiritual life, we must learn how to break our own bones. Francis of Assisi called the rule of his community the "marrow of the gospel." In other words, we must be made of some pretty tough stuff in order to tap into the deeper things of the spirit. We must be willing to experience sacrifice, pain, and even death in order to be born again.

Perseverance is one aspect of stability in monastic life. To remain stable in one's vocation to live in a monastery under a rule and an abbot or abbess until death is no small thing. But it is one of the only ways to discover the deeper treasures of the monastic life. It takes patience, fidelity, questioning, and courageous perseverance. We, too, need patience and perseverance in our own life to live from our inner hermit and make the world our cloister. But we can do it.

With patience we also discover when it is time to move on in our practice. The things that sufficed at the beginning develop as we change spiritually. In monastic life those who first learn to live in the responsibility of strict community life can move on to greater periods of solitude, and even on to complete reclusion. Those who learn to pray the Psalter in the Divine Office for years can often move on to a more meditative approach to praying the psalms in solitude. Those who initially focus on ascetical disciplines move on to sacred reading, and those who find great solace in sacred reading for many years move on to pure contemplation, with little reading or asceticism at all. We never totally give up ascetical disciplines and sacred reading, however. We go beyond but include all such things. In fact, though enjoyed in less quantity, they gain a greater quality as we grow older in contemplation.

But we should not frivolously flit from one thing to another. It is usually best to set a course and stay to it. This includes a daily schedule and a general plan of where we may want to go through the weeks and months ahead. Follow the Spirit's lead. Yes! But we ought not follow our own whims and fancies too easily.

At some point it is helpful to find a good spiritual director to help with this. But, as Saint Seraphim of Sarov advised, better no spiritual director than a bad one. Beyond that, there are the sayings of the fathers and mothers of the church, the teachings of the church, and the kindness and insights of pastors, family, and friends who understand our vocational call as inner hermits.

Give yourself a chance to tap into your desire to be still and make the world your cloister through a habit of prayer. Through perseverance you will grow. Through perseverance in living from your hermit within you will be everywhere without ever leaving your room.

Don't give up. You can do it.

You are doing it right now!

Your Vocation

The call to make the world your cloister by cultivating your inner hermit is a great vocation. It is a state of consciousness rather than a state of life. This means that you can be single or married, with or without children, work in a bank or a field or at a desk in your home, and be faithful to that vocation even if you change your state of life. Things do change, while the inner attitude of contemplative solitude and silence remains stable.

You can be a hermit or a monk, an associate of a community such as Little Portion, or just someone interested in the same values, but you are always aware that "the world is my cloister, my body is my cell, and my soul is the hermit within."

The world changes constantly, even the cells in your body renew themselves all the time, but your inner hermit remains for life, and, after this life, remains in heaven, where it becomes one with God and all God's creation.

Stillness, solitude, meditation, contemplation, praying the psalms, practicing the presence of God, and expressing the virtues are all ways to experience, here and now, that indeed we live and move and have our being in God and with one another.

I pray for your perseverance and your contentment. Please pray for mine. As Saint Julian of Norwich, who changed the world from her own inner hermit, encouraged us, "All shall be well, and all shall be well, and all manner of things shall be well!"

About the Author

John Michael Talbot founded and remains the spiritual father and minister general of the Brothers and Sisters of Charity at Little Portion Hermitage, an integrated monastic community in the Ozark Mountains of Arkansas. A former rock star, he is Catholic music's number one recording artist, with sales of over four million records worldwide. "At the peak of his success, John Michael Talbot was the best-selling male performer in the history of Christian music" (All Music Guide). With more than fifty albums, twenty books, and numerous videos his sold-out concerts are popular among Christians of all denominations throughout the United States. The proceeds often go to Mercy Corps, a Christian world relief agency.

To learn more about the community of the Little Portion Hermitage, see littleportion.org.

To learn more about the ministries of John Michael Talbot, see johnmichaeltalbot.com.